NATIONS of the WORLD

SAMUEL BRIMSON

Library of Congress Cataloging-in-Publication Data available
upon request from publisher. Fax (414) 336-0157 for the attention
of the Publishing Records Department.

ISBN 0-8368-5487-X

This North American edition first published in 2004 by
World Almanac® Library,
330 West Olive Street, Suite 100, Milwaukee, WI 53212 USA.

Created by Trocadero Publishing, an Electra Media Group
Enterprise, Suite 204, 74 Pitt Street, Sydney NSW 2000, Australia.

Original copyright © 2003 S. and L. Brodie.

WORLD ALMANAC® LIBRARY

Ecuador

REPUBLIC OF ECUADOR

Located in northwestern South America, Ecuador borders the Pacific Ocean. It includes the Galapagos Islands, which lie about 600 miles (965 km) off its coast. The western coast is a plain which covers about one-quarter of the country. The Sierra region is made up of two chains of the Andes Mountains. These run through the country from north to south, with a large plateau in between. The eastern landscape features tropical rainforests with rivers feeding into the Amazon basin. Ecuador has continuous hot and humid weather. It is subject to frequent earthquakes..

More than half of the people, have a mixed Spanish and indigenous background. They are called mestizos. Indigenous, Spanish, and African people make up the balance. Most Ecuadorans are Christian. Spanish is the official language. Many indigenous people speak Quechua.

Ecuadorian civilization was an important part of the Incan empire of the late fifteen century A.D. Spanish forces led by Francisco Pizarro arrived in 1532. They executed the Incan emperor, Atahualpa. Several bloody battles followed until the Spanish secured control.

The Spanish established a settlement at Quito in 1534. Explorers had no success in finding gold or other mineral wealth in the area. However, Spanish migrants established prosperous farms. Ecuador was part of the viceroyalty of Peru for nearly three hundred years.

The colonialists staged a revolt against Spain to break its monopoly on trade in 1509. The revolt was put down by Spanish forces. Merchant rebels sought the aid of revolutionary Simon Bolívar. His army, under General Antonio Jose de Sucre, defeated the Spanish at the Battle of Pichincha in 1822.

Ecuador had twenty-one different governments from 1830 to 1895. Most were controlled by conservative landowners from the Andean region.

The Liberal Revolution of 1895 launched a new era under President Eloy Alfaro. He improved civil rights, health care and education. Alfaro, who had attempted to reduce the power of the Catholic Church, was assassinated in 1912.

Major economic and social problems and provoked a military coup d'état in 1925. Isidro Ayora was installed as president, but the situation deteriorated further. From 1931 to 1940 twelve different presidents held power. A coup in 1944 saw José Maria Velasco Ibarra become leader. He was deposed three years later.

Liberal President Galo Plaza Lasso began a program of polit-

Maypole dancers at a festival in Quito, Ecuador's capital city.

FLAT EARTH PICTURE GALLERY

Across the rooftops of Quito.

ical and economic reform in 1948. Velasco Ibarra returned the presidency in 1952. Julio Arosmena Monroy succeeded him in 1960. He was ousted after a 1963 military coup.

Civilian government returned in 1968, with Velasco again president. Beset by economic problems and public protests, he dissolved Congress and established a dictatorship in 1970. The military deposed him two years later. Relations between Ecuador and the United States soured following disputes over fishing rights on the Pacific coast.

The army remained in power until 1979 when Jaime Roldós

Aguilera was elected president. Strict controls were introduced to improve the economy, but none had any lasting effect. Conservative leadership continued under President León Febres Cordero. Cordero was kidnapped and beaten by rebels in 1987.

Ecuador was seriously harmed by a deadly earthquake in 1987. As many as 4,000 people were killed. Damage to Ecuador's main oil pipeline cost nearly a billion dollars in oil revenue.

Sixto Durán Ballén, who became president in 1992, began privatizing state-owned enterprises. He also reached an agreement with international financiers about payment of the country's debts. A group of indigenous people was given rights to a section of rainforest in the east after staging a revolt.

A drop in oil prices and high inflation plunged the nation into crisis during 1999. Strikes and protests prompted the government to declare a state of emergency. Gustavo Noboa Bejarano became president in 2000. The Ecuadorian Congress made the United States dollar the national currency in an attempt to stabilize the economy.

GOVERNMENT
Website www.mmrree.gov.ec
Capital Quito
Type of government Republic
Independence from Spain
May 24, 1822
Voting
Universal adult suffrage,
compulsory
Head of state President
Head of government President
Constitution 1996
Legislature
Unicameral National Congress
Judiciary Supreme Court
Member of
IMF, OAS, UN, UNESCO, WHO,
WTO

LAND AND PEOPLE
Land area 105,037 mi
(272,045 sq km)
Highest point
Chimborazo 20,561 ft (6,267 m)
Coastline 1,390 mi (2,237 km)
Population 13,447,494
Major cities and populations
Guayaquil 2 million
Quito 1.5 million
Ethnic groups Mestizo 55%,
indigenous 25%, African 10%,
European 10%
Religions Christianity 98%,
Languages Spanish (official)

ECONOMIC
Currency US dollar
Industry
petroleum, food processing, textiles,
paper products, wood products,
chemicals, plastics, fishing, timber
Agriculture
bananas, coffee, cocoa, rice,
potatoes, tapioca, plantains, sugar
cane, sheep, pigs, beef, pork, dairy,
balsa, seafood
Natural resources
petroleum, seafood, timber

Egypt

ARAB REPUBLIC OF EGYPT

Egypt includes a large area of northeastern Africa as well as the Sinai Peninsula in Asia. It is bounded by the Mediterranean Sea, Israel, the Red Sea, the Sudan, and Libya. The Nile River and its fertile valley run north to south through the entire country. The river widens into a delta 156 miles (250 km) wide north of Cairo, the capital city. The Aswan High Dam, completed in 1965, regulates the floodwaters that once devastated much of the country each year. Deserts make up more than 90 percent of the country. These deserts include the Sahara, the Arabian, and the Libyan. The Sinai Peninsula is desert in the north and mountainous in the south. Egypt is generally warm to hot in summer and cool to warm in winter.

Most of Egypt's people live in or near the Nile valley and delta. About ninety percent are Hamito-Semitic, descended from the peoples of ancient Egypt. Others come from various nomadic Bedouin tribes such as the Arabdah, Bisharin, Sa'adi and Murabatin.

All but ten percent of the population is Sunni Muslim. There are about two million Coptic Orthodox Christians, as well as smaller numbers of other Christian faiths. Arabic is the official language.

Egypt's economic growth since World War II has been limited because so much money has been spent fighting wars, particularly against Israel. Industrial growth has reduced the country's reliance on agriculture. Many key industries are state-owned. Businesses are gradually becoming free of government involvement, as many adopt a more market-oriented approach. Foreign investment has been increasing steadily.

Farm development was severely limited by the lack of good land prior to constuction of the Aswan Dam. About forty percent of the people work on family farms. The main crops are rice, corn, wheat, beans, cotton, sugar cane, fruits, vegetables and dates. Egypt is presently the largest producer of crops in the world.

Petroleum is the most important mineral product of Egypt. Natural gas is refined on a much smaller scale. Key manufacturing output includes chemicals, fertilizers, clothing, processed foods, textiles, paper products, cement, iron and steel. The primary industrial regions are centered around Cairo, Alexandria and Port Said.

Egypt's current constitution was adopted in 1971. Presidents are nominated by the parliament and approved by the people at a referendum. They serve a six-year term and appoint their own Council of Ministers. Members of the unicameral parliament are elected

A performance of Verdi's opera *Aida* in the spectacular setting of the Cheops pyramid.

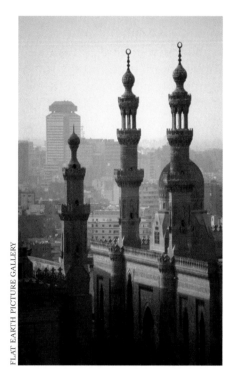

FLAT EARTH PICTURE GALLERY

The smog-shrouded skyline of Cairo.

by the citizens. The Shura, a separate advisory council not officially part of the legislature, has 210 members. Two-thirds of these people are chosen by a vote of the people, while the presidents selects one-third. There are twenty-six local government areas.

Egyptian civilization first flourished between 5000 and 4000 B.C. It was the first politically organized society. Initially there were two kingdoms in the Nile valley. They merged around 3200 B.C. The king was known as Pharaoh.

Historians refer to periods in Egypt's early history as the Old Kingdom, the Middle Kingdom

and the New Kingdom. The Old Kingdom existed until about 2200 B.C. Its leaders were responsible for building the pyramids at Giza. The Middle Kingdom, from 2200 to 1570 B.C., brought greater development. Egypt created a more structured government and built trade ties with Asia.

The New Kingdom, from 1570 to 700 B.C., marked the peak of imperial Egypt. Architecture and art flourished. Egyptian territory spread east as far as the Euphrates River. Egyptian strength went into decline near the end of the New Kingdom.

A succession of weak pharaohs enabled outside kingdoms to conquer Egyptian territories. Assyria took Syria and Palestine while the African Nubians ruled in southern Egypt for a time. Libyans began colonizing the Nile delta.

Persia conquered Egypt in 525 B.C., controlling it until 405 B.C. Alexander the Great took Egypt with little resistance in 332 B.C. Following Alexander's death, Ptolemy I, a general in his army, founded a new Egyptian dynasty. With Alexandria as the center of Egyptian power and culture, the Ptolemys ruled for 200 years.

The Roman Empire developed a strong interest in the thriving country. Octavian (later Emperor Augustus) annexed Egypt in 30 B.C.,

GOVERNMENT
Website www.sis.gov.eg
Capital Cairo
Type of government Republic
Independence from Britain
February 28, 1922
Voting
Universal compulsory adult suffrage
Head of state President
Head of government President
Constitution 1971
Legislature
Unicameral Parliament
People's Assembly (Majlis al-Sha'b)
Judiciary
Supreme Constitutional Court
Member of AL, IMF, OAU, UN,
UNESCO, WHO, WTO

LAND AND PEOPLE
Land area 385,229 sq mi
(997,739 sq km)
Highest point
Mount Catherine 8,625 ft (2,629 m)
Coastline 1,522 mi (2,450 km)
Population 70,712,345
Major cities and populations
Cairo 13.5 million
Alexandria 5.2 million
El Giza 1.7 million
Port Said 0.6 million
Ethnic groups
Hamito-Semitic 90%, others 10%
Religion Islam 90%,
Christianity 10%
Languages Arabic (official)

ECONOMIC
Currency Egyptian pound
Industry
mining, textiles, food processing,
tourism, chemicals, hydrocarbons,
cement, metals
Agriculture
cotton, rice, corn, wheat, beans,
fruits, vegetables, cattle, sheep,
goats
Natural resources
petroleum, natural gas, iron ore,
phosphates, manganese, limestone,
gypsum, talc, asbestos, lead, zinc

Egypt

A vegetable seller at Aswan.

upon the death of Cleopatra. Egypt became Rome's primary source of wheat and other grains. Roman engineers greatly improved the irrigation system.

Coptic Christianity was adopted in the second century A.D. However, when Egypt was invaded by Muslim Arabs in A.D. 639., Christians were forced to pay special taxes.

Years of turmoil followed. Egypt stabilized as the center of trade between east and west under the Fatimids, a Shiite Muslim dynasty. Cairo, founded in 969, quickly became the heart of the nation. Crusades by European Christian kingdoms took a major toll on Egypt. The great warrior Saladin took control of the country and drove

the Christians out in the twelfth century.

For the next three hundred years Egypt was a Sunni Muslim stronghold. The Mamelukes controlled the country erratically until the invasion of the Turkish Ottoman Empire in 1517. The Turks were never able to totally dominate the Mamelukes.

Napoleon Bonaparte of France occupied Egypt in 1798. Claiming he was merely returning it to good order, he left in 1801. His real objective was to cut British supply lines in the Mediterranean. The Ottomans joined with the British to drive out the French. Supported by

The entrance to the Hapshepsut Temple at Luxor.

the Ottomans, Mohammed Ali, an Albanian in the Turkish army, seized power in 1804. He reformed the country's economy and altered the structure of the army. Ali's son, Said, took control and continued development of the country. Said left his successor, Ishmail Pasha, with a country deeply in debt.

Egypt was at the heart of a profound change in world trade when the Suez Canal opened in 1869. The canal was engineered by Ferdinand de Lesseps, and financed by Egypt and France. Weeks were slashed off shipping times between Europe and

Asia. Ismail Pasha was forced to sell Egypt's share in the canal to Britain in 1875 due to the country's huge debt. He was also forced to accept British and French control of Egypt's national budget.

Four years later Ismail abdicated in favor of his son, Tawfik Pasha. Nationalists, angry at the government's weakness, rioted against British and French control. British warships bombarded the city and landed troops, supposedly to restore order. The British consul took charge of Egypt in 1882 after capturing Cairo.

When the Ottoman Empire sided with Austria-Hungary in World War I, Britain declared Egypt a protectorate. Britain promised that the Egyptians would see changes after the war. Independence was granted in 1922. A parliament was established the following year. Problems over Egypt's claims to the Sudan delayed the withdrawal of British troops until 1936. The Suez Canal Zone remained under British military control. Egypt was the scene of a major military campaign to protect the canal from Italian and later German forces between 1940 and 1942.

When Israel came into existence in 1948, Egyptian extremists gained further power, diminishing the authority of King Farouk. Egyptian forces joined other Arab League nations fighting Israel in the southern Negev Desert.

The king was deposed by the military Free Officers' Movement on July 23, 1952. Egypt became a republic under the leadership of General Mohammad Neguiba a year later. His replacement in 1954 was Colonel Gamal Abdel Nasser. A new constitution was proclaimed and Nasser was elected president for a six-year term.

British troops withdrew from the canal zone in June of 1956 under terms of an earlier agreement. Nasser adopted socialist policies, establishing relations with the Soviet Union and receiving its financial aid. Britain and the United States withdrew financing for the construction of the Aswan High Dam on the Nile. Nasser then nationalized the Suez Canal Company, expelling key British officials.

Israel invaded the Sinai region on October 29, 1956, with French and British encouragement. Britain and France landed forces and captured Port Said, at the northern end of the canal. International opposition, led by the United States, forced them to withdraw a short time later. United Nations emergency forces arrived in the canal zone in December following a cease-fire agreement.

The avenue of sphinxes at Luxor.

FLAT EARTH PICTURE GALLERY

Nasser's dream of a united Arab world began to take shape in 1958, when Egypt and Syria formed the United Arab Republic. It broke up three years later. The late 1950s and early 1960s saw substantial industrialization, supported by the Soviet Union. Egypt backed guerrilla activities against Israel and pro-royalist forces in Yemen from 1962 to 1967.

Egyptian forces gathered on the Israeli border in 1967. When Nasser closed the Gulf of Aqaba to Israeli shipping, Israel launched attacks on June 5th.

Egypt

FLAT EARTH PICTURE GALLERY

A ship undergoes repairs in the floating dry dock at Port Said.

The Egyptians were totally overcome within six days. Israeli forces occupied the whole Sinai Peninsula up to the eastern banks of the Suez Canal. Sunken ships in the waterway made it impassable. The canal was not cleared until 1975, depriving Egypt of vast amounts of revenue.

Nasser died in September 1970. His successor, Anwar al-Sadat, freed political prisoners and liberalized economic and social policies. He secretly planned another assault on Israel.

Egyptian forces attacked Israel during the Yom Kippur holiday on October 6, 1973. Recovering, Israeli troops crossed to the west bank of the Suez Canal to cut Egyptian supply lines. Each country made some advances and suffered losses before a peace proposal was signed in late October.

Egypt did not win the war, but it was successful in challenging the Sinai border and regaining control of the Suez Canal. U. S. Secretary State Henry Kissinger provided diplomat aid for the signing of agreements in 1974 and 1975. Egypt reopened the Suez Canal. Israel and Egypt signed a peace treaty in 1979.

Friction between Muslims and Christians led to many arrests and restrictions on the press. Sadat was assassinated in 1981 by extremist members of is army.

Sadat was succeeded by Hosni Mubarak, who restored relations with much of the Arab world while retaining links with Israel. Egypt was invited to rejoin the Islamic Conference in 1984.

Islamic militants continued their attacks throughout the 1990s. When Mubarak committed Egyptian troops to fight against Iraq in the Gulf War, ill-feelings escalated. Sixty-seven foreign tourists were murdered by militants in 1997. Friction continues within Egypt's various political and religious factions, despite a government crackdown. Aided by economic growth within his country, Mubarak was reelected in 1999 for another six-year term.

A Jewish synagogue in Cairo.

FLAT EARTH PICTURE GALLERY

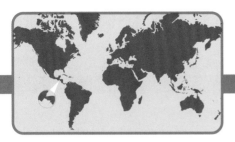

El Salvador

REPUBLIC OF EL SALVADOR

GOVERNMENT
Website www.sv
Capital San Salvador
Type of government Republic
Independence from Spain
September 15, 1821
Voting Universal adult suffrage
Head of state President
Head of government President
Constitution 1983
Legislature
Unicameral Legislative Assembly
Judiciary Supreme Court
Member of
IMF, OAS, UN, UNESCO, WHO, WTO

LAND AND PEOPLE
Land area 8,124 sq mi
(21,041 sq km)
Highest point Cerro El Pital
8,956 ft (2,730 m)
Coastline 190 mi (307 km)
Population 6,353,831
Major cities and populations
San Salvador 500,000
Santa Ana 245,000
San Miguel 185,000
Ethnic groups Mestizo 94%,
indigenous 5%, European 1%
Religions Christianity
Languages Spanish (official)

ECONOMIC
Currency Salvadoran colon
Industry
food processing, beverages,
petroleum, chemicals, fertilizer,
textiles
Agriculture
coffee, sugar, corn, rice, beans,
oilseed, cotton, sorghum, seafood,
beef, dairy
Natural resources
geothermal power, petroleum

The most densely populated Central American country, El Salvador covers about 8,000 square miles (21,000 sq km). It borders Honduras, the Gulf of Fonseca, Guatemala and the Pacific Ocean. A narrow coastal strip runs along the Pacific. Much of the interior of the country is a plateau surrounded by volcanic mountain ranges. Rivers running through the plateau aid in creating some fertile land. Most of the inhabited regions of the country are tropical in climate. They are hot and humid throughout the year, though at higher altitudes they are cooler.

El Salvador suffers from overcrowding because of its large population. More than ninety percent of the people are mestizo, a mix of Spanish and indigenous heritage. Some indigenous people remain. Most Salvadorans are Christian. Spanish is the official language. Indigenous peoples in some regions speak Nahvatl.

Until the sixteenth century, El Salvador was populated by descendants of the Aztecs, known as Pipils. They first migrated to the area in the twelfth century A.D. Spanish forces led by Pedro de Alvarado began forcing indigenous people from their land in 1524. The rich soil soon attracted Spanish settlers who planted coffee and sugar cane.

El Salvador became independent in 1821 as part of the Mexican Empire. When the empire collapsed two years later, El Salvador joined the

The commercial district of San Salvador.

El Salvador

UNITED NATIONS PHOTO LIBRARY

Central American Federation. El Salvador gained its full independence in 1841.

The new country faced ongoing disputes with neighboring countries. Construction of railroads and port facilities proceeded nevertheless. The coffee industry had become very important to the economy. Planters succeeded in having common land ownership by indigenous peoples abolished. As a result, just fourteen families controlled seventy five per cent of the land.

Riding a wave of demands for social change, the Labor Party was elected in 1931. The army deposed it within months. President General Maximiliano Hernández established a dictatorship which lasted until 1944. El Salvador fought with the Allies in World War II. It joined the United Nations in 1945. El Salvador also joined the Organization of American States (OAS) when the organization was founded in 1948.

There was widespread unrest between 1944 and 1950. It ended when Major Oscar Osorio took power, running the country as a dictator until 1956. His successor, Lieutenant Colonel José María Lemus, was deposed in a coup in 1960. Considerable economic progress was made during his term in power. Lieutenant Colonel Julio Adalberto Rivera of the National Reconciliation Party, a front for the army, became president in 1961. Chaos followed his election.

A border dispute with Honduras prompted a brief war in 1969. The activities of left-wing terrorist groups escalated in the 1970s. Government death squads caused havoc, with widespread killings and unrest.

When Col. Arturo Armando Molina was elected in 1972, there were claims that the vote was fraudulent. The same occurred when Gen. Carlos Humberto Romero was elected in 1977. The military overthrew President Romero in 1979, provoking a civil war. Fighting merely increased the following year when Archbishop Oscar Arnulfo Romero was assassinated.

President Alfredo Cristiani, assisted by the United Nations, signed a peace treaty with the rebels in 1991. More than 70,000 people had died in a decade of fighting.

Terrorist activities by both rightist and leftist political movements waned after the 1994 elections. The former left-wing rebels won many seats in the National Assembly in 2000.

El Salvador's economic recovery continues slowly. Some attempts at land reform have been made, but the powerful landowners prevail. Meanwhile, more than fifty percent of Salvadorans live in extreme poverty.

Equatorial Guinea

REPUBLIC OF EQUATORIAL GUINEA

GOVERNMENT
Capital Malabo
Type of government Republic
Independence from Spain
October 12, 1968
Voting Universal adult suffrage
Head of state President
Head of government President
Constitution 1991
Legislature
Unicameral House of
People's Representatives
Judiciary Supreme Tribunal
Member of IMF, OAU, UN,
UNESCO, WHO

LAND AND PEOPLE
Land area 10,831 sq mi
(28,051 sq km)
Highest point Pico Basile
9,868 ft (3,008 m)
Coastline 184 mi (296 km)
Population 498,144
Major cities and populations
Malabo 47,000
Bata 37,000
Ethnic groups
Fang, Bioko and others
Religions
Christianity 90%,
traditional beliefs 10%
Languages
Spanish, French (both official),
indigenous languages

ECONOMIC
Currency CFA franc
Industry
petroleum, mining, fishing,
sawmilling, natural gas
Agriculture
coffee, cocoa, rice, yams, tapioca,
bananas, palm oil, nuts, timber
Natural resources
oil, petroleum, timber,
manganese, uranium

On the southwestern coast of Africa, Equatorial Guinea is a tiny nation of only 10,831 square miles (28,051 sq km). It comprises the mainland Río Muni region plus five islands in the Gulf of Guinea. The coastline is mostly swampland. Dense forests cover the inland plateau. Bioko, the largest island, was formed by ancient volcanoes. It is mountainous and forested with very fertile soil. The climate throughout the country is hot and humid. Rainfall is plentiful.

Most of Río Muni's inhabitants are Fang people. The largest ethnic group on Bioko is the Bubi. Another large group is descended from liberated west African slaves. The dominant religion is Christianity. Spanish and French are the official languages. Languages of the main ethnic groups have also been preserved. The majority of the people work in agriculture.

The island of Bioko was visited by Portuguese navigator Fernando Pó in 1471. It was ceded to Spain along with Río Muni on the mainland in 1778. The Spanish settlers were wiped out by yellow fever in 1781, at which time the region was left to the indigenous peoples. Britain used it as a base for anti-slavery patrols between 1827 and 1844. Liberated slaves were settled on Bioko.

Spain reoccupied Bioko in 1879 as a penal colony for Cubans. The mainland area was officially awarded to Spain at the 1885 Conference of Berlin. It was renamed Spanish Guinea and became a colony of Spain in 1959.

Spain granted the colony internal self-government in 1963. Renamed Equatorial Guinea, it gained independence on October 12, 1968. Francisco Macías Nguema became president. Due to some very strict new policies, most Europeans left within a year.

In 1972 Nguema was declared president for life. His cruel dictatorship forced 100,000 people to flee to neighboring countries. As many as 50,000 are believed to have been killed by the brutal regime. Diplomatic relations with Spain were severed in 1977. Spanish coffee and cocoa planters left the country.

The military executed Nguema during a 1979 coup. He was replaced by Lieutenant Colonel Teodoro Obiang Nguema Mbasogo. Political prisoners were freed and diplomatic ties with European nations were restored.

The regime is still considered oppressive. Most people are unable to improve their lives. Opposition parties frequently boycott elections, claiming that results are being dishonesty manipulated.

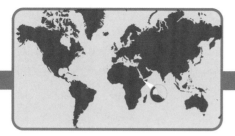

Eritrea

STATE OF ERITREA

Previously part of Ethiopia, Eritrea is in northeastern Africa on the shore of the Red Sea. The central part of the country is rugged plateau land. Much of the coastal strip is desert. More fertile areas can be found in the inland valleys. The climate varies from hot on the coast to cool in the mountains. There is limited rainfall.

Most Eritreans are Afar, Tigray, Tigrinya, Kunama or Saho peoples. A large number are presently living as refugees in Sudan. The population is divided equally between Christian and Muslim. Eighty percent speak Tigrinya or Tigre.

People migrated from northern Africa to the area which is now Eritrea around 2000 B. C. The Aksum kingdom flourished in Eritrea from the first-century A. D. to its peak in the seventh century. Coptic Christianity was introduced in the fourth century A.D. Arab peoples from the eastern side of the Red Sea became dominant in the eighth century. They introduced Islam to the area. Eritrea functioned as a semi-independent state under the authority of Ethiopia.

The Ottoman Empire took control of Eritrea in the sixteenth century. By the nineteenth century Egypt and Ethiopia were locked in a struggle for control of the region. Italy invaded in 1885, declaring Eritrea a colony in 1890. Italy

used it as a base for conquering Ethiopia between 1935 and 1936. Then it was joined with Italian-held Ethopia and Italian Somaliland to form Italian East Africa from 1936 to 1941.

Britain took control from the Italians in 1941. Eritrea became a United Nations trust territory controlled by Britain after World War II. Contrary to Eritrean wishes, the United Nations integrated the country with Ethiopia in 1952.

Eritrean guerrilla groups began battling Ethiopian troops during the 1960s. By 1976 the Ethiopians were so weakened they had to withdraw from Eritrea. They returned two years later, with the assistance of financial aid from the Soviet Union and troops from Cuba. Rebel activity erupted again in the 1980s. The rebels had control of the capital city by 1991.

Eritreans voted overwhelmingly for independence in a 1993 United Nations referendum. Isaias Afwerki became the first president. He privatized state enterprises and encouraged foreign investment.

The border with Ethiopia remains in dispute. In 1998 Ethiopia invaded Eritrea to enforce its version of the border. A United Nations buffer zone was established in June 2000. A peace treaty between Eritrea and Ethiopia came into effect in December.

GOVERNMENT
Capital Asmara
Type of government
Transitional republic
Independence from Ethiopia
May 24, 1993
Voting Universal adult suffrage
Head of state President
Head of government President
Constitution 1993
Legislature
Unicameral National Assembly
Judiciary High Court
Member of
IMF, OAU, UN, UNESCO, WHO

LAND AND PEOPLE
Land area 46,774 sq mi
(121,144 sq km)
Highest point Soira 9,901 ft
(3,018 m)
Coastline 1,388 mi (2,234 km)
Population 4,465,651
Major cities and populations
Asmara 450,000
Ethnic groups
Afar, Tigray, Tigrinya, Kunama, Saho
Religions Islam 50% Christianity 50%
Languages
Various indigenous languages

ECONOMIC
Currency Nakfa

Industry
food processing, beverages, clothing, textiles

Agriculture
sorghum, lentils, vegetables, corn, cotton, coffee, sisal, livestock,

Natural resources
gold, potash, zinc, copper, salt, seafood

Estonia

REPUBLIC OF ESTONIA

Estonia is in northeastern Europe on the Baltic Sea. As well as the mainland, it includes more than 1500 islands in the Gulf of Riga and the Baltic Sea. Most of the landscape is a low plain. Swamps and forests cover major areas, but there are substantial good farmlands. Winters are very cold. Summers are cool to warm.

Over seventy percent of Estonians live in urban areas. Sixty percent are of Estonian background, while thirty percent are Russian. There are Russian, Ukrainian and Finnish minorities. Christianity is the dominant religion. Estonian is the official language.

Service industries such as communication, education, and transportation employ about half of the people. Most of the others work in oil shale mining or farming. Grains and vegetables are the primary crops.

It is believed that Estonians have inhabited the region for thousands of years. Danes and Germans conquered the pagan Estonians beginning in the twelfth century. Christianity was introduced in the 1500s.

Northern Estonia became part of Sweden in 1561. The south was briefly annexed by Poland, and then Sweden. Russia gained control under the treaty of Nystad in 1721.

Peasants were given the right to own land by the mid-1800s. This provoked a growth in Estonian nationalism. Moves for independence peaked in the early twentieth century.

Estonia declared its independence in February of 1918, following the Russian Revolution. Germany, refusing to recognize this, occupied the country. After an invasion by the Germans was repelled, Russia recognized Estonian independence.

Between 1918 and 1933 twenty separate coalitions tried, with limited success, to govern the nation. Konstantin Pätts, who seized power in 1933, ruled as a dictator for five years.

Soviet forces occupied Estonia in 1940. Elections were held, but only Soviet-backed candidates were allowed to run. The Estonian Soviet Socialist Republic was established on August 6, 1940.

Germany invaded in 1941, remaining for three years. There was large-scale immigration of Russians into Estonia following the war.

Soviet leader Mikhail Gorbachev's wide-ranging reforms in the 1980s enabled Estonians to declare the 1940 annexation invalid. A new constitution came into effect in 1992 and Soviet troops withdrew in 1994. With the privatization of state industries, economic aid flowed from the European Union. Development of a market economy has progressed steadily.

Ethiopia

PEOPLE'S DEMOCRATIC REPUBLIC OF ETHIOPIA

Ethiopia is located in the Horn of Africa, in the northeast of the continent. Dominating the landscape is a mountainous plateau split diagonally by the Great Rift Valley. The Blue Nile River has its source at Lake Tana in the north. The highlands and the Blue Nile valley are very fertile. The higher levels of the plateau have a temperate climate. In the lowlands the weather is hot and humid.

The major ethnic groups are the Oromos and Somalis of the southeast, the Amhara in the central plateau and the Tigrayans of the north. Afars populate the northeast, near the Eritrean border. Ten per-cent of the people follow animist religions. The rest are an equal number of Christians and Muslims. Almost all of the Falasha Jewish minority were moved to Israel in the 1980s. Amharic is the official language, but more than 100 dialects are also spoken.

Archeologists have found evidence of human life in Ethiopia dating back 1.5 million years. The Punt people occupied the region after 2000 B.C. Trade with Arabia began around 500 B.C. The Aksum kingdom emerged around 200 A.D. and grew in strength until the tenth century.

Ethiopia is the oldest independent nation in Africa. It converted to Christianity in the fourth century. Some of the population converted to Judaism two hundred years later. Aksum declined in the seventh century after trade links with Byzantium were severed.

From the tenth to the thirteenth century the Zagwe dynasty ruled. It was deposed in 1270 by the Amhara. There was constant war with Oromo infiltrators from the south. Invading Somalis were repelled with Portuguese support in 1520. Ethiopia was financially

United Nations personnel patrolling the buffer zone between Ethiopia and Eritrea in 2000.

devastated by these conflicts. Control was split between Tigrayan and Oromo princes. Neither could protect the land against Egyptian invasions.

Emperor Tewodros II began a program of modernization when he came to power in 1855. He imprisoned several British officials, hoping to gain military aid. Britain sent armed forces to rescue the hostages in 1868 and the emperor committed suicide. Emperor John IV took his place. The new emperor's forces were successful at repelling another invasion in 1875. The emperor was subsequently killed when his forces defeated the Soudanese in the battle of Metamma in 1889.

New emperor Menelik II conducted a successful program to modernize the government and military. He moved the capital to Addis Ababa in 1889. Italian forces invaded Ethiopia in 1895 due to disputed wording in a treaty it had signed with Emperor Menelik II. They were defeated by Menelik's forces in March of 1896.

Emperor Lij Iyasu came to power in 1913. He was deposed in 1916. The emperor was replaced by Menelik's daughter, Zauditu. Following her death in 1930, Ras Tafari Makonnen was crowned as Emperor Haile Selassie I.

Italy invaded Ethiopia in October of 1935. Haile Selassie fled the country the following May. Ethiopia, Italian Somaliland and Eritrea became Italian East Africa. When British forces drove the Italians out in 1941, the emperor returned.

Ethiopia received substantial foreign aid after World War II, but economic development was limited. Most land was owned by a small number of people. The majority of the population remained very poor. Haile Selassie was removed during a military coup in 1974.

A military government was set up under Lt. Colonel Mengistu Haile Mariam. The opposition was wiped out in bloody purges and property was confiscated. Military aid flowed in from the Soviet Union and Cuba supplied troops. Ethiopia became a Communist state in 1984.

Mengistu was unseated by rebel groups in the early 1990s. A transitional government was established. The new repulic held multi-party elections after which Meles Zenawi became prime minister in 1995. Many members of the Mengistu government and the military were tried for genocide in 1996.

Between 1998 and 2000 Ethiopia went to war with Eritrea over a disputed border. Thousands were killed or displaced. A United Nations ceasefire led to the establishment of a buffer zone between the two countries in December of 2000.

GOVERNMENT
Website www.ethiospokes.net
Capital Addis Ababa
Type of government Republic
Voting Universal adult suffrage
Head of state President
Head of government Prime Minister
Constitution 1994
Legislature
Bicameral Parliament
House of People's Representatives (lower house), House of Federation (upper house)
Judiciary Federal Supreme Court
Member of IMF, OAU, UN, UNESCO, WHO

LAND AND PEOPLE
Land area 435,606 sq mi (1,128,176 sq km)
Highest point Ras Dashan 15,158 sq mi (4,620 sq km)
Population 67,673,031
Major cities and populations
Addis Ababa 2,200,000
Dire Dawa 170,000
Harar 140,000
Ethnic groups
Oromo 40%, Amhara & Tigrayan 31%, Sidamo 9%, Shankella 6%, Somali 6%, Afar 4%, others 4%
Religions Christianity 45%, Islam 45%, traditional animism 10%
Languages
Amharic (official), Arabic, indigenous languages

ECONOMIC
Currency Birr
Industry
food processing, beverages, textiles, chemicals, mining, cement
Agriculture
cereals, coffee, oilseed, sugar cane, potatoes, hides, cattle, sheep, goats
Natural resources
gold, platinum, copper, potash, natural gas

Fiji

REPUBLIC OF THE FIJI ISLANDS

Formed largely by ancient volcanoes, 300 islands or islets in the southern Pacific Ocean make up the Republic of Fiji. About one-third of the islands are inhabited. The landscape of the two main islands features fertile coastal plains and river deltas. Inland regions are mountainous and covered with rainforests. The climate is tropical with heavy rainfall between December and April.

The population is fifty percent ethnic Fijian and forty-five percent Indian. There are also European and Chinese minorities. Over fifty percent are Christian and most of the others are Hindus. English is the official language.

Melanesian peoples have lived in Fiji since 1000 B.C. Dutch explorer Abel Tasman was the first European to see Fiji in 1643. He was followed by British navigator Captain James Cook in late 1774.

European traders established a settlement at Levuka. They were followed by British Methodist missionaries. The following years saw prolonged tribal wars and abuses of forced laborers by European planters. Britain annexed the islands in 1874, at the request of tribal chiefs.

Fiji was an important supply station for the Allies during World War II. Various military installations were constructed there. Fijians served in the British forces during the war.

Independence came on October 12, 1970, as a member of the Commonwealth of Nations, with the British monarch as head of state. Fijian tribal chief Ratu Sir Kamisese Mara was the first prime minister.

Mara was defeated in 1987 by Indian-based political parties. Ethnic and religious tensions resulted in a military coup led by Colonel Sitiveni Rabuka. Dissatisfied with progress in giving ethnic Fijians political control, Rabuka staged a second coup in September. He made Fiji a republic and ended membership in the Commonwealth of Nations.

Rabuka was elected prime minister in 1992. Parliament passed measures to protect the rights of ethnic minorities. Following constitutional amendments in 1997, Mahendra Chaudry became Fiji's first Indian prime minister.

Businessman George Speight and his followers stormed the parliament in 2000, taking Chaudry hostage. Speight was arrested and charged with treason. The military took over the government and Laisenia Qarase, an ethnic Fijian, was appointed prime minister. Fiji has been readmitted to the Commonwealth of Nations.

GOVERNMENT
Website www.fiji.gov.fj
Capital Suva
Type of government Republic
Independence from Britain
10 October 1970
Voting Universal adult suffrage
Head of state President
Head of government Prime Minister
Constitution 1990, amended 1997
Legislature
Bicameral Parliament
House of Representatives (lower house), Senate (upper house)
Judiciary Supreme Court
Member of CN, IMF, SPF, UN, UNESCO, WHO, WTO

LAND AND PEOPLE
Land area 7,078 sq mi (18,333 sq km)
Highest point Tomanivi 4,340 ft (1,323 m)
Coastline 702 mi (1129 km)
Population 856,346
Major cities and populations
Suva 210,000
Lautoka 55,000
Nadi 32,000
Ethnic groups
Fijian 50%, Indian 45%, others 5%
Religions Christiaity 53%, Hinduism 38%, Islam 7%, others 2%
Languages
English (official), Fijian, Hindi

ECONOMIC
Currency Fiji dollar
Industry
tourism, sugar, clothing, copra, mining, timber
Agriculture
sugar cane, coconuts, tapioca, rice, sweet potatoes, bananas, cattle, pigs
Natural resources
timber, seafood, gold, copper

Finland

REPUBLIC OF FINLAND

GOVERNMENT
Website virtual. finland.fi
Capital Helsinki
Type of government Republic
Independence from Russia
December 6, 1917
Voting Universal adult suffrage
Head of state President
Head of government Prime Minister
Constitution 1919
Legislature
Unicameral Parliament (Eduskunta)
Judiciary Supreme Court
Member of CE, EU, IMF, OECD, UN, UNESCO, UNHCR, WHO, WTO

LAND AND PEOPLE
Land area 130,556 sq mi
(338,139 sq km)
Highest point Halti 4,357 ft
(1328 m)
Coastline 670 mi (1,126 km)
Population 5,183,545
Major cities and populations
Helsinki 550,000
Espoo 204,000
Tampere 190,000
Vantaa 172,000
Ethnic groups
Scandinavian-Baltic 99%,
indigenous 1%
Religions Christianity
Languages
Finnish, Swedish (both official)

ECONOMIC
Currency Euro
Industry
metal products, mining, electronics,
shipbuilding, pulp and paper,
copper refining, foodstuffs,
chemicals, textiles, clothing
Agriculture
barley, wheat, beet sugar, potatoes;
dairy
Natural resources
timber, copper, zinc, iron ore, silver,
seafood

Finland is located in northern Europe. It has some most unusual geographical traits. The southeastern inland area is an immense, heavily forested plateau. Here, more than 60,000 lakes of varying sizes account for ten percent of the nation's area. Many are linked by rivers, giving Finland an excellent commercial waterway system. The northern third of the country, known as Lapland, lies within the Arctic Circle. Jutting out into the Baltic is an archipelago made up of about 6,500 islands. Most of the people of Finland live in the low-lying southern and western coastal regions.

Finnish winters, which last at least six months, are very cold. This is especially true in Lapland. The short summers, from May to July, are usually pleasantly mild. Thirty percent of the annual rain falls as snow.

Most Finns are of Scandinavian-Baltic heritage. Christianity is the dominant religion, with most people belonging to the Evangelical Lutheran Church. Finnish and Swedish are the official languages. There are several dialects, including Lappish.

Finland had many serious economic problems at the end of World War II. The country had become too dependent on agriculture. Finland has worked to build its manufacturing industries since that time. It now earns considerable income from iron and steel production, shipbuilding, electronics, machinery, chemicals, transportation equipment, and processed foods. Finland is one of the world's largest producers of cellular telephones.

Agriculture still provides about ten percent of Finland's income. Oats, wheat, barley, hay, beet sugar, rye and potatoes are the main crops. Finland's vast forests have provided the resources for thriving wood and paper products industries. Fishing is also an important part of the nation's economy.

FLAT EARTH PICTURE GALLERY

Buying fish at a Helsinki open-air market.

Finland

FLAT EARTH PICTURE GALLERY

One of the many large ferries that link Finland with other Baltic countries.

Finland is a republic operating under a constitution adopted in 1919. The president is elected for a six-year term by a vote of the people. The unicameral parliament is called the Eduskunta. Its members are elected to four-year terms. The cabinet, headed by the prime minister, is appointed by the president with the approval of the Eduskunta.

When the northern ice cap receded around 8000 B.C., the first inhabitants moved into what is now Finland. They were nomadic hunters and gatherers from Asia who eventually became the Lapps. People who became Finns are thought to have come from beyond the Baltic Sea. The Lapps moved farther north as the Finns began to dominate the south in the first century A.D.

The Vikings, from Sweden, made attempts at colonization in the ninth century A.D. Swedish missionaries brought Christianity in the eleventh century. Sweden, the Teutonic Knights, Novgorod and Denmark were all competing for control of the region at the same time. Eventually, with a 1323 treaty, Sweden gained control over most of Finland.

The people of Finland were given the same rights as those in Sweden. Lutheranism, introduced during the sixteenth century, became the dominant Christian faith. Finland was involved in ongoing wars between Russia and Sweden in the latter part of the 1500s.

The Great Northern War of 1700-21 between Sweden and Russia ended with the Treaty of Nystad. Large areas of Finland

The caption for the ferry image reads: **One of the many large ferries that link Finland with other Baltic countries.**

were given to Russia. Additional Finnish territories were conquered by Russia. Finland was left alone to develop its own culture and system of government. Finnish was declared the official language in 1863.

Tsar Nicholas II of Russia began a campaign in 1899 to make Russian culture dominant. He was concerned about growing Finnish nationalism. Russia imposed new limits on the rights on the Finns. When Russia went to war against Japan in the early 1900s, focus shifted away from Finland. A desire for independence brought demands from the Finns. Concessions, including universal adult suffrage and a unicameral parliament, were made in 1906.

Finland's leaders declared the country independent on December 6th, 1917, at the outbreak of the Russian Revolution. The Russian Bolshevik army stormed into Finland, plundering towns and killing civilians. Marshal Carl Gustav Mannerheim and his Finnish White Guard, supported by Germany, began its own assault on the Russian troops. The Russians were driven out within five months.

The Republic of Finland was declared in July of 1919. K. J. Ståhlberg was named president.

The 1920s and early 1930s brought clashes between extremist political movements. Most governments of Finland were unstable.

A 1932 non-aggression pact with the Soviet Union failed to prevent the Soviets invading at the start of World War II. Although Finland was defeated, Finnish resistance movements prevented Soviet forces from occupying the country. The Karelian Isthmus, the Rybachi Peninsula and other lands were ceded to the Soviet Union under the Treaty of Moscow in 1940.

When Germany attacked Russia in June 1941, Finland allied itself with the Germans. Thousands of German troops soon occupied Finland. Russia bombed many Finnish cities. Britain declared war on Finland, and the United States severed relations. Marshal Mannaheim, elected president in 1944, worked for a truce which was signed the same year.

The 1947 Treaty of Paris set Finland's borders as they had been before the war. The Soviets gained a lease on the Porkkala region. Finland was required to pay US.$300 million in reparations to the Soviet Union.

Immediately after the war, Communist Party members were elected to office and occupied senior government posts. Their power waned in the late 1940s as other parties came to power. Finland worked to maintain harmonious relations with the Soviet Union, fearing another invasion. It remained neutral throughout the Cold War.

The Soviet Union became Finland's major trading partner. Following its collapse in the early 1990s, Finland suffered a severe economic downturn. It has since reoriented its foreign relations focus toward the rest of Europe. Economic recovery has been very successful since that time. Finland joined the European Union in 1995.

Senate Square, Helsinki.

France

FRENCH REPUBLIC

GOVERNMENT

Website
www.premier-ministre.gouv.fr/en
Capital Paris
Type of government Republic
Voting Universal adult suffrage
Head of state President
Head of government Prime Minister
Constitution 1958
Legislature
Bicameral Parliament
National Assembly (lower house),
Senate (upper house)
Judiciary Supreme Court of Appeals
Member of CE, EU, IMF, NATO, OECD, UN, UNESCO, UNHCR, WHO, WTO

LAND AND PEOPLE

Land area 210,025 sq mi (543,965 sq km)
Highest point Mont Blanc 15,771 ft (4,807 m)
Coastline 2,129 mi (3427 km)
Population 59,765,983
Major cities and populations
Paris 2,300,000
Marseille 850,000
Lyon 440,000
Toulouse 385,000
Ethnic groups
French 94%, others 6%
Religions
Christianity 90%, Islam 7%, Judaism 1% Buddhism 1%
Languages French (official)

ECONOMIC

Currency Euro
Industry
machinery, chemicals, motor vehicles, metallurgy, aircraft, wine, electronics; textiles, food processing, tourism, mining
Agriculture
wheat, cereals, beet sugar, potatoes, wine grapes, beef, dairy
Natural resources
coal, iron ore, bauxite, zinc, potash, timber, seafood

Located in western Europe, France has two coastlines. The western coast is on the Bay of Biscay and the English Channel. The southern coast faces the Mediterranean Sea. A large part of France is a central plateau and adjoining plains. The Alps and the Jura Mountains form a natural border with Switzerland and Italy. The Pyrenees, in the south, form a border with Spain and Andorra. The major rivers are the Loire, Seine, Rhône and Garonne. European France includes the island of Corsica in the Mediterranean Sea. The country also has several overseas departments, collectives and territories.

The climate in France varies with the regions. Winds from the Atlantic give the northwest warm summers and cool winters. The northeast has a more severe spread of temperatures from summer to winter. In the south, winters are warm and summers can be very hot. Plentiful rain falls throughout most of the country, most heavily between June and October. France has an odd weather syndrome in the south central region. A violent north wind, called a mistral, commonly blows from the Mediterranean.

Seventy-five percent of France's population lives in urban areas. Paris, with a population in excess of two million, is the only truly large city. Marseille is the only other city with a population exceeding 500,000. All but ten percent of the people have French heritage. Some others have moved from neighboring countries. There is also a significant minority descended from those who migrated from France's North African colonies, especially Algeria.

Around ninety percent of the people are Christian. Of the other ten percent, the largest group is Muslim, numbering over four million. Most other religions and sects are also represented.

French is the official language, spoken by virtually all of the population. The use of regional languages is declining, although Alsatian, Flemish, Basque, Provencal, Corsican and Catalan are spoken in specific areas.

A large portion of the French landscape is devoted to agriculture. Grapes are a very important crop. Many parts of France, particularly in the west, south and southwest, are devoted to wine production. France and Italy lead the world in the production of wine. Other principal crops are beet sugar, wheat, barley, potatoes and corn. Fruits are grown in southern regions. Livestosk includes Cattle, sheep, pigs, goats and poultry.

The French economy depends a good deal on

tourism. In the summer months, the country attracts millions of visitors from all over the world. Paris is a bustling tourist mecca. The Mediterranean coast is lined with popular resorts and holiday homes.

Much of France's heavy industry is located in the north and northeast. There is a substantial motor vehicle industry. Aircraft construction is very important. The Airbus Consortium, a leading aircraft manufaturer, is located in Toulouse. Chemicals, electronics and electronic equipment, clothing and textiles, transport equipment, heavy machinery and food are also key industries. Paris is a center for the production of luxury consumer goods.

France's well-developed transport system includes an extensive rail network. It ranges from local commuter lines to high-speed links to other parts of Europe. The ultra-high-speed Train Grande Vitesse (TGV) links Paris with other major French cities. The Eurostar line runs through the Eurotunnel under the English Channel, connecting France to England. Domestic air services link virtually all medium to large communities around the country. A vast network of

The cathedral of Notre Dame in Paris.

BRAND X PICTURES

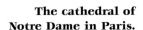

France

AIRBUS INDUSTRIE

An A340 airliner manufactured by Airbus Industrie, Toulouse.

highways and motorways covers the nation.

The present constitution was adopted in 1958, when the Fifth Republic was established. The French president, elected for a five-year term, is head of state. The president is commander of the armed forces and presides over the High Council of the Judiciary, the Committee of National Defense and the Council of Ministers. There is a bicameral parliament made up of the National Assembly and the Senate. The 577 members of the National Assembly are elected by the people for terms of up to five years. The 321 Senators are elected for nine years by an electoral college. The prime minister and cabinet, although appointed by the president, are responsible to the parliament.

The nation has 96 local governing groups called departments. The departments are organized into 22 regions. The overseas departments are French Guiana, Martinique, Guadeloupe and Réunion. They are included in the French electoral system. The two territorial collectivities—Mayotte, and St. Pierre and Miquelon—have a status below that of a full overseas department. The four overseas territories are Wallis and Futuna, New Caledonia, French Polynesia and the French Southern and Antarctic Territories.

Archeological evidence shows that people have lived in the area of France for over 100,000 years. Cave paintings have been found at Chauvet in the Ardeche region and at Lascaux in the Dordogne region,

both in southern France. People living in around 4000 B.C. left many stone monuments in Brittany. Greek explorers reached the Mediterranean coast around 600 B.C. and founded a colony where Marseille is now located.

The country was populated by Celtic peoples known as Gauls, from whom it got its earliest name. They lived in tribes based in separate regions throughout most of the area. Smaller communities of Basques populated the south.

Roman forces commanded by Julius Caesar conquered Gaul between 58 and 51 B.C. It was a Roman province for five centuries. Its capital was Lugdunum, now the city of Lyon. The Romans introduced a formal legal system and brought many social improvements. Christianity became widely accepted after the first century A.D. Gauls fought for Rome in battles against Germanic tribes to the north and east. The Roman Empire's decline in the fourth century A.D. left Gaul exposed to invasion.

Germanic groups swept into Gaul from the northeast. Romans worked to establish alliances with these tribes which included Visigoths, Franks, Burgundians and Huns. The Franks conquered Gaul in 486 A.D., under the leadership of Clovis I. King Clovis I embraced Christianity in 496.

Clovis's Merovingian dynasty held power until 751, but it was in steady decline after Clovis's death in 511. The kingdom was divided between his sons who waged wars for most of the sixth century. Gaul was reunited in 613 under Clotaire II, and maintained by his successor, Dagobert I. The dynasty deteriorated rapidly after King Dagobert's death in 639.

Various regional mayors gained much power during this time. One of these men, Pepin of Herstal, extended authority over much of southern France. His son and successor, Charles Martel, gained huge respect after his defeat of Arab invaders in 732. Martel's son, Pepin the Short, deposed the

last Merovingian king in 751. He begin a line of kings which became known as the Carolingian Dynasty.

Pepin's son, Charlemagne, became King of the Franks in 768. He expanded the realm into German Bavaria and Saxony, forcibly converting them to Christianity. The Pope crowned Charlemagne Emperor of the Romans in 800, making him the most powerful ruler in western Europe. The title had last been held by Romulus Augustulus in 476 A.D.

Charlemagne made major improvements in the legal and

administrative structures of the kingdom. He called upon leading scholars to help him enact educational and religious reforms. Charlemagne was succeeded by his son, Louis I, in 1814. Many problems, including Viking raids, made it difficult for Louis to hold the empire together. He died in 840. His sons—Lothair, Louis and Charles—divided the realm into three competing regions under the 843 Treaty of Verdun.

Louis's territory was the area which is now Germany. Lothair ruled lands where France and Germany now meet. Charles II,

Place de la Concorde, Paris, where many executions took place during the French Revolution.

France

took control of most of the area in present-day France.

Central authority in France was not strong under Charles II. It was replaced by large feudal territories. Powerful nobles such as the dukes of Burgundy and Aquitaine gradually usurped the king's authority. Stronger Viking raids occurred during the ninth and early tenth centuries. West Frankish King Charles III surrendered an area to the Vikings that became known as Normandy.

When the Carolingian Dynasty ended in 987, the nobles chose Hugh Capet as king. This marked the beginning of France as a kingdom separate from areas to the east and north. The Capetians kings wanted to maintain relations with the country's nobles, yet they wanted to build a stronger royal government. King Louis VI built a stronghold of royal power in the Ile-de-France area surrounding Paris. They worked to increase their domain over the powerful nobles who governed specific areas.

William, Duke of Normandy, invaded Britain in 1066. He defeated the forces of King Harold at the Battle of Hastings. The Norman conquest changed the course of British history.William became King William I of England.

Capetian King Philip II, who reigned between 1180 and 1223, extended his domain to include most of France. The power of the nobles was severely curtailed. Paris became a center for Christian learning during the thirteenth century. King Louis IX (1226–1270) was a leader of the Christian crusades against Islamic influence in the Holy Land. He also overhauled the legal system.

King Charles IV died in 1328 without an heir. The crown passed to his nephew, Philip VI, of the Valois branch of the Capetian family. His rule was contested by King Edward III of England, grandson of the French King Philip IV, in 1337. Edward already controlled large areas of France by inheritance.

The dispute between the two kings began the Hundred Years War. The English King Henry V scored a major victory over France at Agincourt in 1415. Five years later King Charles VI of France named Henry V his successor. Henry claimed the throne in 1422 but controlled only a small area of France.

English forces besieged Orléans in 1428. Christian peasant girl Joan of Arc came to the aid of Charles VII as a brave warrior. She rallied his forces and liberated the city. Joan was condemned as a hertic and put to death in 1431, after having begun a valiant struggle. The war continued for another twenty years. The tide turned in 1453 when the Duke of Burgundy changed allegiance from England to France. The French gradually expelled

A centuries-old street in the city of Strasbourg.

The Moulin Rouge nightclub, a landmark in the Montmartre district of Paris.

the English, except for a small enclave at Calais.

Louis XI finally broke the power of the nobles during his reign, from 1461 to 1483. He levied taxes on landowners which helped strengthen his government.

King Charles VIII invaded Italy in 1494, beginning a brutal power struggle that continued until 1559. It brought France into conflict with the powerful Austrian-Spanish Habsburg Dynasty.

The Christian Reformation, begun by Martin Luther in Germany, spread to France and gained many supporters. From

1560 Catholics battled Protestants for control of the kingdom. Protestant Huguenots were widely persecuted until granted permission to worship by the 1598 Edict of Nantes.

The powerful Catholic League forced King Henry IV to convert from Protestantism before entering Paris to take up the crown in 1594. This was the beginning of the Bourbon dynasty.

King Henry renewed the country's economic growth. He offered public lands for sale to citizens at a low cost. He built roads, bridges, and canals. Foreign artisans were brought in to introduce new industries.

King Henry was assassinated in 1610. Some records indicate

that the assassin was sent by the Habsburg.

The reign of his successor, Louis XIII, was notable for the rise of Catholic statesman Cardinal Richelieu. From 1624 to 1642, as the king's chief minister, he was the most powerful person in France. He protected the king from repeated plots by his brother, the Duke of Orléans, to unseat him.

Richelieu took France into the Thirty Years War in 1635 against the Habsburg of Germany. Despite his Catholicism, he allied France with the Protestants of Sweden and the Netherlands. He realized a Catholic victory would enable the Habsburg Empire to threaten France's security. French financial and military aid bolstered the weakening

Narrow alleys in the picturesque village of Eze in southern France.

France

Protestants, bringing victory in 1648.

Louis XIV, the Sun King, came to the throne in 1643, beginning a golden age for France. Louis surrounded himself with many astute advisers. His court at Versailles became a center of power, as well as one of art and culture.

King Louis XIV led wars against Spain and the Netherlands in the 1660s and 1670s, greatly depleting the economy. The War of Spanish Succession was fought from 1702 to 1713 to prevent the Spanish and Austrian thrones reuniting under the Habsburgs. Eventually, in 1714, Louis XIV's grandson ascended the Spanish throne as Philip V.

France clashed with England over colonies in the Americas and India during the Seven Year's War, from 1756 to 1763. France supported Britain's American colonies when they revolted in 1776. All of this encouraged the growing dissatisfaction with the monarchy.

Louis XVI convened the Estates-General on June 17, 1789. This body, made up of nobility, clergy and commoners, was concerned about the country's economy and the vast power of the king. The group renamed itself the National Assembly and set out to write a constitution for France. This was the beginning of the French Revolution.

SCOTT BRODIE

The elegant, ornate Carlton Hotel is at the heart of the Cannes beach resort region.

On July 14, 1789, Parisians stormed the Bastille prison. Peasants all across the country began a revolt against their feudal masters. The National Assembly drafted the Rights of Man document. It seized the property of the church and issued new currency. It reorganized the government and wrote a new constitution.

Louis accepted the new constitution on September 14, 1791. It created a constitutional monarchy and a legislative assembly with 745 members. The king, however, was unwilling to operate under the new constitution. A mob deposed the king on August 10, 1792.

The new assembly became the National Convention, made up of 749 elected officials. It abolished the monarchy and established the First French Republic.

The National Assembly's Comittee of Public Safety, led by Maximilien Robespierre, began the Reign of Terror against aristocrats and opponents of the revolution. King Louis was convicted of treason. His execution in January of 1793 provoked royalist uprisings around the country. The bloodshed continued as thousands were executed. Robespierre's death in 1794 marked an end to the Reign of Terror.

The constitution of August 1795 created a new bicameral parliament called the Directory. The Directory governed France for four years, but Royalists wanted a return to a monarchy. General Napoleon Bonaparte staged a coup on November 9, 1799. He became the First Consul of France, operating on a constitution he had written.

Napoleon's efficient administration cleaned up the worst of the economic crisis. The Code Napoléon, the legal system he created, is the basis of French

Napoleon Bonaparte.

law today. He named himself Emperor of the French in 1804.

Napoleon's armies defeated the Russians and Austrians at Austerlitz in December of 1805. Similar success followed the next year against Prussia at Jena. His campaign against Russia in 1812 resulted in his first disastrous defeat as emperor. Austria and Prussia captured Paris, forcing Napoleon to abdicate in 1814. He was exiled Elba, then escaped in 1815 to lead French armies against the British at the Battle of Waterloo. He was defeated and then sent to an island in the south Atlantic Ocean.

Residences cling to every available space on the steep hills overlooking the Mediterranean Sea in southern France.

Louis XVIII became king, establishing a parliamentary monarchy. He tried to reaffirm the social reforms begun by Napoleon. Charles X, who became his successor in 1824, attempted to reinstate the king's absolute power. This provoked the July Revolution of 1830. He was replaced by Louis-Philippe, the citizen king. Disregard for the poor and growing economic problems combined to end his reign with the February Revolution of 1848.

Louis-Napoleon Bonaparte, nephew of the former emperor, became president of the Second Republic. Four years later he staged a coup to extend his term and create himself Emperor Napoleon III. Prosperity returned, but the regime was repressive and authoritarian. Napoleon III built extensive public works facilities which transformed many cities, especially Paris. He increased trade and improved banking.

France successfully supported Britain against Russia in the 1854–56 Crimean War. Napoleon III attempt to create a Catholic empire in Mexico in 1867 ended disastrously. France's colonial empire did expand considerably in Africa and Indochina.

The 1870–71 Franco-Prussian War ended with Napoleon captured and Prussian, Russian and Austrian forces entering Paris. A settlement required France to pay a huge fee to Germany and to cede it the region of Alsace-Lorraine.

France

France established a new government which became known as the Third Republic. A republican constitution was adopted in 1875. Subsequent governments were unstable but material prosperity continued. Colonial expansion generated friction with Britain and Germany.

Archduke Francis Ferdinand of Austria was assassinated at Sarajevo in 1914, by a Serbian radical. As a result, Austria invaded Serbia. France, Britain and Russia backed Serbia. Turkey and Germany sided with Austria. Full-scale war commenced in August of 1914.

Much fighting took place in northeastern France. More than 300,000 French soldiers died and 600,000 were injured. French troops were joined by British and American forces to oppose Germany.

A peace conference was held at Versailles in 1919. The Allies forced Germany to pay vast reparations. Even so, Clemenceau lost office because he was seen to have been too soft on the Germans. The region of Alsace-Lorraine was returned to France.

The economy of France was devastated after the war. The value of the franc had fallen

dramatically. The 1930s Great Depression caused widespread unemployment. To counter the rise of fascism, the Radical Socialists, Socialists and the Communist Party formed the Popular Front alliance. Led by Léon Blum, they won a majority in 1936. Many pioneering social reforms were enacted.

Blum's successor, Édouard Daladier, participated in the appeasement of Adolf Hitler's Nazi administration at Munich in September 1938. France joined Britain in permitting Germany to occupy part of Czechoslovakia.

Germany invaded Poland in September 1939. France and Britain came to Poland's defense, as earlier promised. German forces had overrun France by June of 1940. Paris was declared an open city to

avoid its destruction. Marshal Henri Philippe Pétain signed an armistice. He was the new figurehead of the Vichy government. It governed the half of France not occupied by Germany.

French General Charles de Gaulle established an organization, Free France, and a government-in-exile in London. When Allied forces secured control of North Africa in late 1942, de Gaulle moved his base to Algiers.

Across France, determined resistance movements harassed the Germans. They supported the Allies by operating extensive intelligence networks. The Allied invasion force landed at Normandy in northwestern France on June 6, 1944. Paris was liberated on August 25th.

France, Britain, the United States and the Soviet Union occupied Germany.

France became a charter member of the United Nations in 1945, including a permanent seat on the Security Council. De Gaulle established a government in 1945, but he stepped down as leader a year later. A new constitution was approved in 1946, creating the Fourth Republic. The new French Union included France and its many colonies.

Many economic and social reforms took place after the war. Key industries were nationalized and reconstruction was a priority. A huge amount of aid flowed in from the United States under the Marshall Plan.

Colonial matters occupied much time in the 1950s. Communist Viet Minh, led by Ho Chi Minh, controlled the non-urban areas of Vietnam. A large and well-equipped French army was humiliated by the Viet Minh at the Battle of Dien Bien Phu in May 1954. France withdrew from Indochina soon afterward.

The French minority in Algeria was determined that Algeria would remain part of France. Nationalists were equally determined to gain independence. The conflict resulted in civil war. The French military staged a coup in Algeria in 1958.

Charles de Gaulle was invited to become president. He answered the nation's call on October 5, 1958. Under a new constitution, the Fifth Republic was created, with greatly increased presidential powers. De Gaulle reorganized the French Union into the French Community. The colonies could vote for continuing association with France or independence. Most chose the latter in 1960.

Algeria remained a huge problem. Right-wing military officers formed the Secret Army Organization (OAS). They conducted a terror campaign to force the retention of Algeria as part of France. Determined not to be cowed, de Gaulle granted Algeria independence in 1960. He was widely condemned by right-wing elements.

France participated in forming the Common Market, which later became the European Union. De Gaulle withdrew France from the North Atlantic Treaty Organization to end the impression of dependence on U. S. military strength.

Students at the University of Paris staged an immense protest in 1968. This led to

The architecture of the La Defense district of Paris is in stark contrast to the rest of the city.

France

nationwide demonstrations by students and workers. Violence erupted as protestors clashed with police. The situation became so critical, for a time it seemed the French government would collapse.

DeGaulle dissolved the parliament and called for new elections. His Gaullist Party won the first absolute majority in French parliamentary history. When de Gaulle's proposals for reforms were defeated in a 1969 referendum, he resigned.

Georges Pompidou, prime minister from 1961-68, was elected president in June of 1969. He maintained an independent foreign policy, but dropped deGaulle's opposition to Britain joining the Common Market. Pompidou instituted many tough proposals for aiding the deteriorating economy.

Valéry Giscard d'Estaing was elected president after Pompidou's sudden death in 1974. It was a time of rising inflation and unemployment caused by the oil crisis. Giscard's tough austerity measures led to his defeat in 1981.

President Francois Mitterand was the country's first elected Socialist. He began a program of social welfare reforms. He nationalized banks as well as major industries, while expand-ing social benefits and job opportunities.

A right-wing coalition under Prime Minister Jacques Chirac won power in the parliament in 1986. Ultra-right wing National Front members were elected for the first time. Chirac called for privatization of many state-owned enterprises.

Mitterrand was forced into a run-off election in 1988 when ultra-right wing, anti-immigration politician Jean-Mari Le Pen won a large number of votes. Although Mitterrand won, he modified his socialist program. France contributed substantially to the Gulf War against Iraq in 1990–91, despite the fact that it had previously maintained close ties with Iraq.

Mitterrand remained in office through the mid-90s, despite health problems. Rising unemployment brought large street demonstrations by industrial and agricultural workers. Prime Minister Alain Juppé's plans to restructure the social security system also caused widespread industrial action.

The victor at the 1995 presidential election was conservative Jacques Chirac. He retained the presidency in 2000 over Jean-Marie Le Pen. Most sides of French politics rallied against Le Pen, enabling Chirac to secure a substantial victory.

France showed its willingness to cooperate with the rest of Europe by endorsing the euro as its currency, effective in 2002. The military draft was abolished the same year, in favor of a smaller, volunteer army.

The skyline of Lyon in central France.

French Overseas Territories

French Guiana

French Guiana is on the northern coast of South America. Its original inhabitants were Carib, Arawak, Wayana, Oyampi and Palicur peoples. Settlers from France arrived in 1637 but it was not until the 1713 Treaty of Utrecht that French possession was confirmed. Slaves were imported from Africa to work the plantations.

A penal colony for French convicts was established in 1852. It became notorious for its brutality. With the founding of the Fourth Republic in 1946, Guiana became a French overseas department with representation in the French parliament.

During the 1970s and 1980s there were calls for greater autonomy. Pro-independence demonstrations in Cayenne turned violent in 1999. French Guiana is the location of the Arianespace consortium's rocket launching facility.

Guadeloupe

Guadeloupe is a group of islands in the Caribbean Sea off the northeastern coast of South America. They were originally inhabited by Arawak and Carib peoples. A French group began growing sugar cane using slave labor imported from Africa in 1635.

France annexed Guadeloupe in 1674, making it a dependency of Martinique. British forces occupied the islands in the mid-1700s and again in the early 1800s. Guadeloupe and Martinique became separate colonies in 1775. With the founding of the Fourth Republic in 1946, Guadeloupe became a French overseas department with representation in the French parliament.

The 1960s and 1970s were a time of upheaval, with demands for independence or greater autonomy. Most active were the socialist and communist political movements. Agitation for independence continues today.

Martinique

Martinique is in the southern Windward Islands in the eastern Caribbean Sea. It was originally inhabited by Arawak and Carib peoples. French settlers arrived in 1635 and began displacing the indigenous peoples. They established large sugar cane and coffee plantations. African slaves were imported as laborers.

Britain occupied the islands briefly in 1762–63 and in the early 1800s. After the Napoleonic Wars, Martinique was confirmed as French territory in 1816. A violent eruption of Mount Pelée completely destroyed the town of Saint-Pierre in 1902.

With the founding of the Fourth Republic in 1946, Martinique became a French overseas department with representation in the French parliament. Paris granted increased autonomy in 1982. Independence demands have been muted since that time.

Réunion

Réunion is part of the Mascarene Islands group, in the Indian Ocean east of Madagascar. It was first visited by the Portugese in the early sixteenth century. A French trading company annexed it under a royal charter in the mid-1600s. Settlers arrived in the early 1700s to grow coffee and other crops for the nearby island of Mauritius. Slave labor was imported from Madagascar.

France abolished slavery in 1848. Planters wanting to maintain slavery launched an independence movement. Unable to gain control, they imported indentured laborers from India to grow sugar cane.

With the founding of the Fourth Republic in 1946, Réunion became a French overseas department with representation in the French parliament. Local communists have worked for greater autonomy or independence. French Prime Minister Michel Rocard's visit in 1991

French Overseas Territories

was greeted by violent riots. Complete self-government while remaining associated with France is now the aim of most of the island's residents.

TERRITORIAL COLLECTIVITIES

St. Pierre and Miquelon

These two tiny islands are located off the southern coast of Newfoundland in the north Atlantic Ocean. Mostly barren rock, they were uninhabited when Portuguese mariners arrived in 1520. A French fishing settlement was established in 1604. Refugees from Britain's occupation of French Canada swelled the population in the early 1700s. After the Napoleonic Wars, they were restored to France in 1814.

Free France troops occupied the islands during World War II. St. Pierre and Miquelon became a French overseas department in 1976 and a territorial collectivity in 1985. Recent history has centered on disputes with Canada over fishing rights.

Mayotte

Mayotte is an island in the Indian Ocean near Comoros, east of Africa. Malay people first inhabited the island in the sixth century A.D. Mayotte became an Islamic sultanate when Arab traders established bases there.

Annexed by France in 1843, it was grouped with other Comoros Islands in 1912. With the founding of the Fourth Republic in 1946, Mayotte became a French territorial collectivity, a status below that of an overseas department.

Calls for independence in the 1970s clashed with demands for continued association with France. Mayotte refused to become part of Comoros in 1978. Economic problems plagued Mayottte in the 1990s, provoking riots. Nonetheless, in 2000 seventy percent of voters favored maintaining links with France. Comoros persists in striving to gain Mayotte as part of its country.

OVERSEAS TERRITORIES

French Polynesia

French Polynesia comprises 100 islands in the southeastern Pacific Ocean. Polynesian peoples settled the islands 2000 years ago. Europeans arrived in 1767. Following the visit of HMS Bounty to the islands in 1789, sailors mutinied against Captain William Bligh's authoritarian leadership. The London Missionary Society preached Christianity to the islanders from 1797.

France annexed the islands in 1842, against stiff opposition from the Polynesians. They became a French overseas territory in 1957. Mururoa Atoll was used for testing French nuclear weapons in the 1960s and 1990s, despite widespread international condemnation. French President Jacques Chirac announced in 1996 that no more tests would be made.

French Southern and Antarctic Territories

This territory includes the Crozet and Kerguelen islands in the south Indian Ocean, plus the Antarctica territory claimed by France. The claim on Antarctica is not recognized by most nations. A permanent scientific research base was established in the Kerguelen Islands in 1950. The French Southern and Antarctic Territories was created in 1955. Previously, the various islands had been administered as part of Madagascar.

New Caledonia and Dependencies

This group of islands is in the south Pacific Ocean east of Australia. Grand-Terre is the large main island. Kanak people first settled the islands around 4000 BC. Captain James Cook surveyed the islands in 1774, giving them their name. Annexed by France in 1853, they were made a dependency

of Tahiti. They were made a separate administration in 1884.

Most land was allocated to French settlers and the Kanaks were confined to reservations. Allied military forces used the islands as a base during World War II. They became a French overseas territory in 1946.

During the 1980s the Kanak FLNKS independence group was involved in armed confrontations with French forces. The large French-descended population wants union with France while the Kanaks want independence. Greater autonomy has been granted and Kanaks now play a more prominent role in government.

Wallis and Futuna

These volcanic islands are in the southern Pacific Ocean between Fiji and Samoa. They were first settled more than 2000 years ago by Polynesian groups from neighboring islands. France annexed Wallis in 1886 and Futuna the following year. The islands became a colony in 1924.

Allied military forces were based on Wallis during World War II. Wallis and Futuna became an overseas territory in 1959. Futuna attempted to have the territory split into two separate entities in 1983. There is no strong independence movement.

Gabon

GABONESE REPUBLIC

Gabon is on the Atlantic coast of west central Africa. Dominating its coastline is the wide Ogooué River estuary. From the coast the land rises slowly to the central plateau. Two mountain ranges cross the plateau. The climate is constantly hot and humid with plentiful rainfall.

The population comprises more than forty distinct ethnic groups, all of Bantu origin. The largest are the Fang, Eshira, and Adouma. Europeans, mostly French, make up a small but highly visible minority. Nearly forty percent of the people follow traditional animist religions. Most of the rest are Christian. French is the official language, but various Bantu dialects are also spoken.

There is evidence humans lived in Gabon during the Stone Ages. Little is known about who they were. Bantu groups appeared during the first century A.D. The now-dominant Fang arrived in the eighteenth century, with the intention of trading with Europeans.

The Portuguese established a lucrative slave trade in 1843. The French navy controlled the region from 1843 to 1886. They attempted to eliminate the slave trade. Libreville was founded in 1849 as a settlement for freed slaves.

Gabon became a full colony as a part of French Congo in 1886. It became part of French Equatorial Guinea from 1910 to 1957. Medical missionary Albert Schweitzer established a hospital on the banks of the Ogooué in 1913.

Gabon was held by the Free French during World War II. It was made a French Overseas Territory in 1946. Twelve years later it became internally self-governing as part of the French Community. Independence was gained on August 17, 1960, with Leon M'ba as president.

A 1964 coup d'état was suppressed by French troops. Following Mba's death in 1967, his successor, Omar Bongo, created a one-party state. Bongo was able to overcome most opposition by creating a booming economy. Foreign investors became partners in Gambonese development during the 1970s. Oil, natural gas, uranium, and manganese became profitable exports. President Bongo has been reelected six times.

Anti-Bongo movements reached a peak in 1989 with seven days of bloody rioting at Port Gentil. President Bongo permitted the formation of new political parties the folllowing year.

There were regular charges of electoral fraud throughout the 1990s. Bongo and his party continued to win with healthy majorities. Gabon enjoys a relatively healthy economy and is one of Africa's most prosperous countries.

GOVERNMENT
Capital Libreville
Type of government Republic
Independence from France
August 17,1960
Voting Universal adult suffrage
Head of state President
Head of government Prime Minister
Constitution 1991
Legislature
Bicameral Parliament
National Assembly (lower house),
Senate (upper house)
Judiciary Supreme Court
Member of IMF, OAU, UN, UNESCO, WHO, WTO

LAND AND PEOPLE
Land area 103,347 sq mi (267,667 sq kn)
Highest point Mont Iboundji 5,167 ft (1,575 m)
Coastline 550 mi (885 km)
Population 1,233,353
Major cities and populations
Libreville 375,000
Port Gentil 85,000
Ethnic groups
Fang 30%, Eshira 25%, others 40%
Religions Christianity 60%, traditional animism 39%, Islam 1%
Languages
French (official), indigenous languages

ECONOMIC
Currency CFA franc
Industry
food, beverage, textiles, timber products, cement, mining, oil refining, chemicals, ship repair
Agriculture
cocoa, coffee, sugar, palm oil, rubber, cattle, forestry, seafood
Natural resources
petroleum, manganese, uranium, gold, timber, iron ore

The Gambia

REPUBLIC OF THE GAMBIA

A long and narrow country, The Gambia stretches to the east for 200 miles (320 km) from the Atlantic Ocean on the western coast of Africa. It follows the Gambia River. At no point is the country more than 30 miles (50 km) wide. From the sandy beaches of the coast the land rises only slightly and much of it is covered with grassland or swamp. The climate is subtropical, with a wet season from June to October. The land is not ideal for many kinds of farming. Peanut farming, however, largely supports the country's economy.

The Mandinka, Fula, and Wolof, as well as many smaller ethnic groups, account for ninety-five percent of the population. The majority are Muslims. English is the official language although Arabic is widely used. Various dialects are spoken by the different ethnic groups.

Iron work found in the area indicates a society in about 800 A. D. Ancestors of the present peoples began arriving in the thirteenth century. The Mali Empire controlled the region for the next two hundred years. The Portugese were the first Europeans to reach the region in 1455. They began early trading stations along the river. French and English traders replaced the Portugese in the seventeenth century.

The British lieutenant-governor of Sierra Leone established the town of Bathurst (now Banjul) at the mouth of the Gambia River in 1816. Traders followed, establishing settlements inland. There was rapid development of the peanut growing industry. Most of the crop was exported to Europe.

Governed from Sierra Leone, The Gambia was declared a British protectorate in 1894. It was controlled by local chiefs supervised by British commissioners after 1902. Britain began educational and political improvements after World War II. The Gambia became independent on February 18, 1965, as a member of the British Commonwealth. Dawda Jawara was its prime minister. The people voted in favor of a republic in 1970 and Jawara was elected president. A 1981 coup d'etat failed due to military aid from Senegal. This led to a confederation with Senegal which lasted until 1989.

In the midst of a 1994 economic downturn, army officers led by Lieutenant Yahya Jammeh overthrew Jawara. Voters approved a new constitution establising a multiparty system. Jammeh was elected president in 1996 and again in 2001. Both elections were marred by charges of fraud. Jammeh and his party, The Alliance for Patriotic Reorientation and Construction, continue to rule.

Georgia

REPUBLIC OF GEORGIA

Georgia is in southeastern Europe on the eastern shore of the Black Sea. Its northern boundary is primarily the Caucasus Mountains. The Lesser Caucasus Mountains make up much of the south and central parts of the country. The climate varies a good deal, from humid and subtropical along the coastline to drier and colder temperatures in the east.

Ethnic Georgians make up a large part of the population. Other smaller groups include Russians, Armenians, Azeri and Ossetians. Half the population lives in urban areas. Most of its Christian majority belong to the Georgian Orthodox Church. The official language is Georgian, but many people speak Russian.

Ionian Greeks colonized Georgia in the sixth century B.C. Georgia became formalized as a kingdom in the fourth century B.C. Conversion to Christianity occurred in the fourth century A. D. The Persians and the Byzantines fought for control of the area for many years.

The Arabs ruled beginning in the seventh century, followed by the Turks in the eleventh century. King David II expelled the Turks in the twelfth century, reviving Georgia as an independent kingdom. Both Persia and the Ottoman Empire ruled parts of Georgia through the mid-1700s, when a new kingdom was proclaimed.

Georgia was incorporated into the Russian empire in 1801. It became independent during the Russian Revolution in May of 1918.

The Soviet army invaded Georgia in February of 1921. It was combined with Armenia and Azerbaijan as the Soviet Transcaucasian Republic in 1922. It became part of the Soviet Union in 1936.

Calls for independence returned in the late 1980s as the Soviet Union began to crumble. Georgia declared its independence in April of 1991. Its first president, Zviad Gamsakhurdia, was deposed within a year. Eduard Shevardnadze, former Soviet foreign minister, returned to his homeland to rebuild the government. Shevardnadze and a new parliament were elected the following fall.

Abkhazia, an area in northwestern Georgia, began asserting its own independence in 1991. The government of Georgia refused to acknowledge this demand. Hundreds of thousands of ethnic Georgians were forced from Abkhazia. A similar rebellion was held by Ossetians in yet another area of the country. These rebellions continue.

Shevardnadze has escaped two assassination attempts, most recently in 1998. The country remains in cooperation with Russian troops stationed at four Georgian bases.

GOVERNMENT
Website www.parliament.ge
Capital T'bilisi
Type of government Republic
Independence from Soviet Union
April 9, 1991
Voting Universal adult suffrage
Head of state President
Head of government President
Constitution 1995
Legislature
Unicameral Supreme Council
(Umaghiesi Sabcho)
Judiciary Supreme Court
Member of
CIS, IMF, UN, UNESCO, WHO, WTO

LAND AND PEOPLE
Land area 26,900 sq mi
(69,700 sq km)
Highest point
Mt'a Mqinvartsveri 16,558 ft
(5047 m)
Coastline 193 mi (310 km)
Population 4,989,285
Major cities and populations
T'bilisi 1,400,000
K'ut'aisa 255,000
Rust'avi 161,000
Ethnic groups Georgian 70%,
Armenian 8%, Russian 6%,
Azeri 6%, Ossetian 3%
Religions Christianity 75%
Islam 11%
Languages Georgian (official),
Russian

ECONOMIC
Currency Lari
Industry
steel, aircraft, machine tools,
electrical goods, mining, chemicals,
wood products, wine
Agriculture
citrus, grapes, tea, vegetables,
potatoes, livestock
Natural resources
forests, manganese, iron ore, copper

Germany

FEDERAL REPUBLIC OF GERMANY

GOVERNMENT
Website www.bundesregierung.de
Capital Berlin
Type of government Republic
Voting Universal adult suffrage
Head of state President
Head of government Chancellor
Constitution 1949
Legislature
Bicameral Parliament
Federal Assembly (Bundestag)
Federal Council (Bundesrat)
Judiciary Federal Constitutional
Court
Member of CE, EU, G-10, IMF,
NATO, OECD, UN, UNESCO,
UNHCR, WHO, WTO

LAND AND PEOPLE
Land area 137,735 sq mi
(356,733 sq km)
Highest point Zugspitze 2963 m
Coastline 9,718 ft (2,962 m)
Population 83,251,851
Major cities and populations
Berlin 3.5 million
Hamburg 1.8 million
Munich 1.3 million
Cologne 1 million
Frankfurt am Main 0.7 million
Ethnic groups
Germans 90%, Turks 2%
Religions Christianity 75%, Islam
2%
Languages German (official)

ECONOMIC
Currency Euro
Industry
tourism, mining, iron, steel,
cement, chemicals, machinery,
motor vehicles, machine tools,
electronics, food, beverages;
shipbuilding; textiles, electrical
goods
Agriculture
potatoes, wheat, barley, beet sugar,
fruit, cattle, pigs, poultry, grapes
Natural resources
iron ore, coal, potash, timber,
lignite, uranium, copper, natural
gas, salt, nickel

Germany is a republic in central Europe. It is bordered by France, Belgium and the Netherlands on the west, Denmark on the north, Poland and the Czech Republic on the east, and Austria and Switzerland on the south. Its two coastlines face the North Sea in the northwest and the Baltic Sea on the north.

The German landscape has three distinct regions. The low-lying North German Plain dominates the north. It rises to no more than 300 feet (appr. 100 m) above sea level. Its dominant waterway, the River Elbe, flows northwest. The central uplands include low mountains, river valleys and numerous basins. Much of this area is heavily forested. The industrial complexes of the Ruhr, Main and Hesse regions are found here. The Rhine and Main rivers cross through this region. The Jura Mountains dominate the southwest, while the Bavarian Alps form the extreme south central border.

The climate is temperate throughout most of Germany. The Baltic and North seas bring highly variable temperatures to the north. In the east and the south, winters can be very cold. Summers across the country are generally cool to warm.

The population is largely ethnically German. There are, however, significant minorities from Turkey, Italy, Greece, Poland, Spain and the former Yugoslav republics. Many arrived during the 1970s economic boom. Germany passed restrictions on immigration in the early 1990s, but those limits were lifted in 1999.

Christianity is very strong in Germany. The north is primarily Protestant, while Catholicism prevails in the south and west. There is a significant Muslim minority. The Jewish population is now less than 40,000 people. In what used to be East Germany, more than half the population claims no religious affiliation. The government provides financial

Public transport in Düsseldorf.

FLAT EARTH PICTURE GALLERY

Germany

support for churches through a special tax levy on their behalf.

The official language is German. There are several regional dialects including Allemanic, Franconian and Plattdeutsch. The Serbs and Danes still speak their own languages.

Germany has a highly educated workforce. As a result, it has one of the world's most prosperous economies.

Manufacturing forms the core of Germany's economy. Major products include iron and steel, motor vehicles, transportation and industrial equipment, chemicals, electronics, ships, food products, petrochemicals and textiles.

Germany continues to face a particular challenge since the early 1990s. Prior to the fall of the Berlin Wall, West Germany was far more technologically advanced than East Germany. The country is working to upgrade manufacturing capabilities in the east.

Service industries are thriving in Germany. Outstanding among these is banking and related financial services.

Agriculture is built around crops such as beet sugar, wheat, vegetables, barley, cabbage, fruit and dairy products. Cattle and pigs are extensively farmed. There is a large and thriving wine industry.

Germany's mineral resources are limited. While it does mine coal, lignite, iron ore, and potash, other minerals are imported. Forestry provides a good deal of income for the country, as does fishing.

Germany is a federal republic with sixteen states. The national parliament is made up of two houses. The Bundesrat, or upper house, has members elected from each state according to population. Members of the Bundestag, or lower house, are elected by a mixed proportional and direct system, for four years.

The head of government, the chancellor, is elected by the Bundestag by an absolute majority for a four-year term. The president, as head of state, is elected for five years by a special federal convention made up of the Bundestag plus an equal number of delegates

The spectacular Neuschwanstein Castle at Schwangau.

BRAND X PICTURES

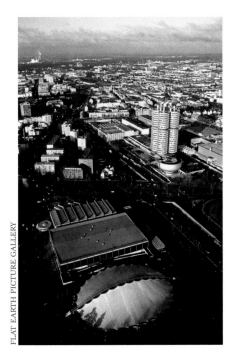

The BMW motor vehicle factory and headquarters in Munich.

elected from the state parliaments. The president is primarily a figurehead with no influence on government.

The national government handles defense, foreign relations and finance. Most other matters are controlled by the states, each of which has its own parliament.

The single nation of Germany, as it exists today, is a relatively recent creation. The first human inhabitants roamed the land during the Old Stone Age some 400,000 years ago. The region was inhabited by Germanic and Celtic tribes after 2000 B.C. The Germans gradually became dominant.

The Germanic people came into conflict with the Roman Empire beginning in the second century A.D. Rome already held the territory west of the River Rhine and south of the Danube. It attempted, unsuccessfully, to expand its territory as far east as the River Elbe.

The Romans were, at first, successful in maintaining a border at the Rhine and Danube rivers. However, beginning in the fourth century, various Germanic tribes swept into the Roman Empire. They entered Gaul, as France was then called, and by the fifth century had established the Frankish Empire.

The Franks were united under King Clovis I in 486 A.D. His domain encompassed southern and western Germany and much of France. He converted to Christianity in 496 and established the Merovingian dynasty. After the death of King Dagobert I in 639 the dynasty deteriorated rapidly.

Pepin the Short, having deposed the Merovingian king in 751, declared himself ruler. Pepin's son, Charlemagne, became King of the Franks in 768. He expanded the realm into other parts of Germany, plus Bavaria and Saxony. All were forcibly converted to Christianity.

The pope crowned Charlemagne Emperor of the West in 800. This title derived from the old Roman Empire and had not been used since 476 A.D. It made him the most powerful ruler in western Europe.

The Treaty of Verdun separated Franconia from the Frankish Empire in 843. Franconia became the Kingdom of the Eastern Franks, ruled by Louis the German. This was the beginning of Germany as it is today.

The kingdom was divided between his sons after Louis' death in 876. Emperor Arnulf reunited it between 887 and 899. His son, Louis the Child, reigned from 900 to 911. The kingdom suffered repeated Viking, Slav and Magyar invasions. The centralized kingdom collapsed and power passed to regional nobles.

Franconia, Upper Lorraine, Lower Lorraine, Swabia, Bavaria and Saxony became the most powerful duchies. They elected Conrad I as king in 911. Much of his time was spent trying to control the powerful dukes while fighting off Magyar invasions.

Henry, Duke of Saxony, was elected King Henry I in 918. During his reign royal authority over the dukes increased. He engineered the election of his son as King Otto I in 936. Otto set out to revive the policies of Charlamagne. Pope John XII, in recognition of this endeavor, crowned Otto as Holy Roman Emperor in 962.

Germany

**Wine grapevines at
Überlingen — Germany
is a major wine producer.**

Most German kings were crowned Holy Roman Emperor from this time on. One struggle for this title took place between King Henry IV and Pope Gregory VII beginning in 1076. The pope refused to install him as emperor because Henry had interfered in the appointment of bishops. Henry proceeded to depose Pope Gregory in favor of Pope Clement III, who crowned him emperor in 1084.

King Frederick I Barbarossa, who reigned from 1152 to 1190, successfully challenged papal powers. He also broke the power of the last independent duchy, Saxony-Bavaria. Those who followed him as monarch were less successful.

Germany's existence as a single entity was shaky. It advanced to the nineteenth century as a collection of separate states, cities and regions. This, however, did not hamper the expansion of German territory or commercial interests. The Hanseatic League, a trade union of north German cities, became very strong in the thirteenth century. It expanded into most regions surrounding the Baltic Sea, gaining both wealth and power.

The Teutonic Knights were formed during the Siege of Acre in the Holy Land in 1190–91. It was a monastic order with strong military overtones. Holy Roman Emperor Frederick II granted them substantial privileges in 1226. In the thirteenth century, working for Poland, the Knights conquered Prussia. Grand Master Hermann von Salza began a campaign to make Prussia a separate German state. The order expanded north into Baltic and Scandinavian territories.

The election of kings was often manipulated by powerful duchies. When the Hohenstaufen dynasty ended in 1254, Rudolf of Habsburg was elected King of the Germans. He became Holy Roman Emperor in 1273. This brought Germany under the influence of the Austrian Habsburg dynasty, which would last 600 years.

Germany in the 1400s and 1500s was the site of a number of revolutionary developments. Johannes Gutenberg became the first European to develop a printing process using movable type in 1448.

Martin Luther, an Augustinian monk and university professor, began challenging the Roman church in 1517. He became outraged by the church's system of 'indulgences', which were a guarantee of entry to heaven given to wealthy or influential people by the pope. They made large donations to the church in return. Luther began publishing leaflets about indulgences.

When Luther questioned the pope's infallibility, he offended the church hierarchy, but his thoughts were widely applauded in Germany. Powerful supporters gave him protection from Rome's wrath. Luther translated the Bible from Latin into German. This made it available to anyone who could read, eliminating the need for interpretation by priests.

Luther's actions set off the Reformation which split Roman Christianity into Catholic and Protestant. It prompted a violent revolt by German peasants in 1524. The movement spread west and north and across to Britain.

Growing Protestant power alarmed Catholic Habsburg Austria. The Habsburgs launched the Counter-Reformation. This led to the Thirty Years War beginning in 1618. When the Protestants were losing in 1635, help came from an unexpected source. Catholic Cardinal Richlieu, the French king's principal minister, committed French troops and money to the Protestant side. He was concerned that a victorious Habsburg Empire could invade France.

Peace came in 1648, but Germany was devastated by the conflict. Germany deteriorated once more into a weak confederation. A large portion of the population fled the country. Many more starved.

The German states were once again gaining power by the seventeenth century. Austria and Prussia had become major competitors. Prussia, under Frederick the Great, took Silesia from Austria during the 1740–48 War of the Austrian Succession. Frederick went on to prove Prussia's superiority over Austria in the Seven Years War, from 1756 to 1763. Prussia and Austria divided Poland between them in 1772. Frederick the Great had become very powerful. He was primed to challenge the Habsburg's control of Germany.

The French revolutionary period after 1789 brought many changes to Germany. Prussian

Martin Luther.

forces were decisively defeated by Napoleon's army at Jena in 1806. Napoleon reconstituted Western Germany as sixteen states. Long overdue reforms changed the social and administrative structure. He dealt the final death blow to the Holy Roman Empire, which had been in decline for many years.

Following Napoleon's defeat, the 1815 Congress of Vienna created a new German Confederation under Austria's control. It followed much the same structure Napoleon had established. This came about because of the masterly diplomatic skills of Prince Clemens Metternich.

Metternich was determined to restore Austria's prestige after its humiliation at Napoleon's hands. An alliance with Prussia prevented revolutionaries from gaining inde-

Traditionally dressed musicians at Rothenburg.

Germany

FLAT EARTH PICTURE GALLERY

Mounted police patrolling in front of Berlin's Brandenburg Gate, which once marked the border between East Berlin and West Berlin.

the Industrial Revolution. Manufacturing thrived, as did agriculture aided by new machines. Bismarck crushed Catholic opposition to his leadership by establishing civilian authority over marriage and other ceremonies. He resigned in 1890 due to disagreements with both the Roman church and the growing Socialist Party.

Germany began aggressively acquiring colonies in Africa and the Pacific after 1884. Germany's international commerce began to rival that of Britain. Its navy was capable of challenging the powerful navy of Britain by the end of the century. Germany's relations with France and Britain had steadily deteriorated. By contrast, those with Austria-Hungary and the Turkish Ottoman Empire had improved.

A Serbian revolutionary assassinated Archduke Franz Ferdinand of Austria-Hungary in June of 1914. Events moved swiftly as Austria-Hungary declared war on Serbia. Russia mobilized its forces against Austria-Hungary. This prompted Germany to declare war on Russia and France. German forces moved into France, entering Belgium to get there.

pendence for the other German states.

When Otto von Bismarck became chancellor of Prussia, he provoked the Austro-Prussian War of 1866. He was determined to create a 'Little Germany', while excluding Austria completely. Victorious Prussia created the North German Confederation, ending Austria's domination. Prussia's

victory in the Franco-Prussian War of 1870–71 produced a similar result with France.

Wilhelm I of Prussia became the German kaiser, or emperor. France ceded the Alsace-Lorraine region to Germany. Germany began an rapid rise to economic dominance of Europe.

Although he was very conservative, Bismarck encouraged

This violation of Belgian neutrality brought Britain into the war on France's side.

For the next four years, Germany was bogged down in a horrendous war fought on both eastern and western fronts. Successes against Russia aided revolutionaries in overthrowing its czar in 1917.

The confrontation with the armies of France and the British Empire killed millions. Most fighting took place in northern France and southern Belgium. Exhausted by war and economically unsound, Germany sued for peace in late 1918. The war ended with an armistice on November 11th.

The 1919 Treaty of Versailles put enormous pressure on Germany. It was forced to make payment to the victorious nations over the next several years. All German colonies were forfeited and much of its industry was dismantled. The industrial Rhineland became a demilitarized zone. Terrible hardship marked the following years, largely because of the monetary settlements being paid. French and Belgian troops occupied the Ruhr area when Germany defaulted on its payments in 1923.

A new constitution was adopted at Weimar in 1919. The Germany it created was called the Weimar Republic, a much more centralized and cohesive structure. Social Democratic president Friedrich Ebert put down a communist uprising the same year he took office. The uprising was an attempt to create a Soviet republic in Bavaria.

Political radicals on both the left and right were tearing the country apart. The years 1922–23 were the worst. Ebert weathered an attempted takeover by Adolf Hitler's National Socialists and destabilizing tactics by the Bolsheviks.

When Ebert died in 1925, he was replaced as president by Field Marshall Paul von Hindenburg. Hindenburg successfully engineered coalitions which included the German People's Party, the Catholic Center Party and the Social Democrats.

A period of relative stability followed. Negotiations led to an easing of the reparations payments. Stringent economic measures brought rampant inflation under control and the currency stabilized. Germany was admitted into the League of Nations in 1926 as it began a slow return to prosperity.

Recovery halted in 1930 when the world economic depression set in. Mass unemployment fuelled the rise of radical political parties. On one side was the Communist Party, on the other the National Socialists, or Nazis, led by Adolf Hitler. The Nazis became the largest party in the Reichstag, displacing the Social Democratic majority in 1932.

Berlin's memorial to people killed while trying to cross the Berlin Wall from east to west.

Germany

Hindenburg tried numerous methods to avoid appointing Hitler as chancellor. Nazis staged violent street protests. Their intention was to show the nation was ungovernable unless Hitler became chancellor. Hindenburg bowed to the increasing pressure and appointed Hitler in January of 1933. At the same time he appointed a non-Nazi cabinet to act as a buffer.

Hitler used the burning of the Reichstag building in Berlin on February 27, 1933 as an excuse to assume emergency powers. He called new elections the following month. The Nazis gained forty-three per cent of the vote. Legislation was passed greatly enhancing the chancellor's powers and dimishing those of the president. Hitler was now a virtual dictator.

Changes came rapidly after this. Hitler made Germany a one-party state. He began cracking down on labor unions and communists. He terminated membership in the League of Nations. Hindenburg's death in August of 1934 paved the way for Hitler to assume the presidency as well. He was named Führer, or leader, of the Third Reich, as the German Empire was now called.

A cargo barge passes through the city of Frankfurt on the River Main.

Hitler had already brutally purged the party of all opponents. As head of state and head of government, as well as commander of the military, he had absolute power. A master of inspirational rhetoric, Hitler promised the German people an empire which would last one thousand years. It would be a worthy successor to the Holy Roman Empire. Joseph

Goebbels elevated Hitler to near divine status by manipulating all national media.

Hitler brought order and economic growth to the nation. Money was pumped into the economy through major state building projects. Young people were organized into semi-military organizations and the Gestapo secret police suppressed any dissent.

The Bavarian Alps are popular with walkers during the summer months.

A campaign against Germany's Jews began in earnest in 1934. Claiming they were responsible for Germany's economic problems, the Nazis passed the Nuremberg Laws. Jews were stripped of citizenship, banned from most professions and forbidden marriage to non-Jews.

Hitler began rebuilding the German military machine in defiance of the Treaty of Versailles. German forces reoccupied the Rhineland in 1936. That same year he negotiated an alliance, the Axis, with fascist governments in Italy and Japan. Germany provided valu-able assistance to the fascist General Franco during the Spanish Civil War.

By 1938, Hitler's ambitions had spread beyond Germany. German forces occupied Austria, incorporating it into the Third Reich in March. Britain and France concluded the Munich Agreement with Hitler in September 1938, hoping to avoid another war in Europe. It allowed Germany to occupy the German-speaking Sudetenland region of Czechoslovakia.

By March of 1939, all of Czechoslovakia was under Nazi control, as were parts of Lithuania. The western Europeans were shocked when the Soviet Union and Germany signed a non-aggression pact in August 1939.

Germany had been forcibly negotiating with Poland for access to the Baltic port of Gdansk. The Soviet pact allowed Hitler to pursue a more aggressive course of action, the invasion of Poland. Britain and France demanded the forces be withdrawn. When this did not happen, both declared war on Germany on September 3rd.

Superbly equipped German forces swept through Poland, Norway, Denmark, the Netherlands, Belgium and into France. Paris fell in June of 1940. German forces reached the English Channel, poised to invade Britain.

In the east, German forces swept into Yugoslavia and Greece. They inflicted terrible defeats on British and Commonwealth forces in April of 1941. Hitler ignored the pact he had made with the Soviet Union and invaded in June of 1941. German forces were able to reach Moscow, but were ultimately repelled. Twenty million people died.

When Italian forces collapsed in North Africa, Germany's took their place. A monumental desert campaign ensued across Libya and Egypt. British forces ultimately prevailed in 1942, dealing the Germans their first major defeat.

The process of eliminating Jews and other minorities began once the invaded areas had been secured. Millions were rounded up across eastern and western Europe, then shipped to German concentration camps. Many were executed, while others were imprisoned or forced into labor camps.

Italy was invaded by the Allies in 1943. Italian forces were defeated by June. German forces occupied the north of Italy, holding the invaders at bay. German cities and industrial complexes were under constant bombardment by British and United States air

Germany

forces by this time. The Soviet Red Army was advancing from the east. United States and British troops staged massive landings at Normandy in June of 1944. A plot by German military officers to assassinate Hitler failed the following month.

The Allies had pushed German forces across the border into Germany by February of 1945. With the Third Reich on the verge of collapse, Hitler committed suicide in Berlin on April 30, 1945. Germany signed an unconditional surrender agreement at Rheims in France seven days later.

East Prussia and Silesia were handed over to Poland.

The Saarland was taken by France. The rest of Germany was divided into four zones of occupation by the United States, Britain, France and the Soviet Union. Berlin, although located within the Soviet zone, was similarly divided. Many Nazis were tried and executed for war crimes. The Nazi Party was banned.

Germany became the central battleground of the ensuing Cold War. Until 1947 Germany faced famine because of poor harvests. This was complicated by vast numbers of refugees escaping the Soviet zone of occupation.

The three non-Soviet occupying powers included West Berlin in currency reform proposals in 1948. When the Soviets blockaded access to Berlin, the Berlin Airlift of 1948–49 followed. Vast numbers of transport aircraft maintained a continuous shuttle service into West Berlin. This kept the city supplied with food and other necessities. Specific road access corridors ultimately were agreed upon.

The nation became firmly divided into East and West Germany. East Germany was the German Democratic Republic, under communist control. West Germany, the Federal Republic of Germany, comprised the

Medieval buildings in the marketplace at Rothenburg.

Adolf Hitler.

British, United States and French zones and a free market economy.

The two Germanys developed separately through the 1950s. Large numbers of East Germans and Poles escaped into West Germany until the construction of the Berlin Wall in 1961. Their skills contributed enormously to its industrial rebirth. Bonn became West Germany's capital. Christian Democrats led by Konrad Adenaeur won the first postwar elections in 1949.

The Allies formally occupied Germany until 1955. Under the Paris Agreements of 1954, West Germany once again became a sovereign nation. Its capacity to rearm or possess chemical, biological or nuclear weaponry was severely restricted. United States aid, under the Marshall

FLAT EARTH PICTURE GALLERY

ELECTRA COLLECTION

Plan, greatly assisted the rebuilding.

In East Germany the Socialist Unity Party held power from October 1949. It was a brutal Stalinist regime. A workers' uprising in 1953 was crushed by Soviet military forces. Efforts to expel Britain, France and the United States from West Berlin began after 1958.

When this failed, the Party constructed the notorious Berlin Wall, sealing the western section off from East Germany. Heavily fortified, it effectively halted the exodus of East Germans to the west. Similar barriers soon lined the full length of the border between East and West Germany.

The 1960s and 1970s were marked by widespread protests and terrorist activities in West Germany. Radical left-wing groups such as Baader-Meinhof and the Red Army Faction pursued their goals with violence. There were also mass demonstrations against the war in Vietnam.

At the 1972 Munich Olympic Games, Arab terrorists of the Black September organization took Israeli athletes hostage. Both hostages and kidnappers died in a failed rescue attempt.

The Social Democrats came to power in 1969. Willy Brandt was chancellor. German indus-

The spectacular architecture of Lubeck.

Germany

try was fully recovered and once more exporting to the world. Germany's economy grew immensely from the 1950s to the 1980s.

Mikhail Gorbachev's extensive reforms in the Soviet Union after 1985 were not welcomed in East Germany. Events, however, overtook the leadership of Erich Honecker. When the border with Czechoslovakia was opened in 1989, refugees poured out of East Germany.

Encouraged by Gorbachev, East Germans staged large and widespread demonstrations. Acts of civil disobedience began once the demonstrations had been crushed. Moves for a new administration were led by the citizen's group called New Forum.

When Honecker resigned in October 1989 he was replaced by Egon Krenz. Half a million people turned out to protest in East Berlin in November. The government began reorganizing. Restrictions on foreign travel were lifted and the border was opened to millions of people. The demolition of the hated Berlin Wall began.

In West Germany, Chancellor Helmut Kohl secured an agreement for reunification of the two Germanys. The first free elections were held in East Germany in 1990. The legislatures of East and West agreed to monetary, social and eco-

nomic union effective June 1st. The Soviet Union agreed to withdraw its forces from the East by 1994.

Elections were held for a united Germany in December of 1990, for the first time since 1933. Kohl became chancellor of the new Germany. Germany's economy was under enormous strain as old and inefficient industries in the East were integrated with those of the West throughout the 1990s. Differences in social programs from East to West have caused some dissatisfaction with the reunification process.

The weakened economy necessitated strict spending cuts. Fascist groups were on the rise again by the late 1990s. Attacks were made on foreign guest workers. Social Democrat Gerhard Schröder was elected chancellor in 1998, leading a liberal coalition government.

Most of the government's functions had left Bonn by 2000. Berlin was once again Germany's capital. Massive redevelopment has wiped out much of the evidence of the time of division and the hated wall has long since disappeared.

Frankfurt am Main is the major financial center of Germany.

Ghana

REPUBLIC OF GHANA

GOVERNMENT
Website www.ghana.gov.gh
Capital Accra
Type of government Republic
Independence from Britain
March 6, 1957
Voting Universal adult suffrage
Head of state President
Head of government President
Constitution 1992
Legislature Unicameral
Parliament
Judiciary Supreme Court
Member of
CN, IMF, OAU, UN, WHO, WTO

LAND AND PEOPLE
Land area 92,100 sq mi
(238,537 sq km)
Highest point Mount Afadjato
2,903 ft (885 m)
Coastline 335 mi (539 km)
Population 20,244,154
Major cities and populations
Accra 3,000,000
Kumasi 700,000
Tamale 300,000
Ethnic groups
Akan (Fante & Anshanti) 40%,
Moshi-Dagomba 17%,
Ewe 14%, Ga 9%, others 20%
Religions
Christianity 28%, Islam 30%,
traditional animism 30%
Languages
English (official), indigenous
languages

ECONOMIC
Currency Australian dollar
Industry
tourism, mining, agriculture, motor
vehicles, steel, food processing,
chemicals
Agriculture
wheat, barley, sugar cane, fruits,
beef cattle, sheep, wool, poultry,
dairy
Natural resources
gold, timber, diamonds, bauxite,
manganese, seafood, rubber

Ghana is located in western Africa. The Atlantic Ocean coastline is marked by sandbars and lagoons. The coastal plain is crossed by many rivers and streams. The enormous Lake Volta, created by damming the Volta River in 1964, is one of the largest artificial lakes in the world. The land rises steadily to form ranges of hills on the east and west. The climate is hot and humid throughout the country, somewhat drier in the north.

More than seventy-five percent of Ghana's people live in the southern half of the country. The Fanti and the Ashanti are the largest of Ghana's seventy-five ethnic groups. Both are descended from the Akan people. The north is dominated by the Moshi-Dagomba. The country is almost evenly divided among Christians, Muslims, and those who follow animist beliefs. Most Muslims live in the north. While English is the official language, several indigenous languages are also spoken.

The economy of Ghana has several diverse elements. About sixty percent of the population works in agriculture, growing cocao, coffee, bananas, tobacco and different kinds of nuts. Forests cover about one-third of the land. Wood and paper products account for substantial income. The mining of gold, manganese, bauxite and diamonds also brings significant income to the country.

Ghana once included several kingdoms which developed between the thirteenth and fifteenth centuries A.D. Gonjan and Dagomba ruled in the north, Fanti and Ashanti in the south.

Portuguese slave traders established a settlement at Elmina in 1482. The region became known as the Gold Coast. The Ashanti cooperated enthusiastically in supplying the Portuguese with slaves. They later expanded their dealings to include British, Dutch and Danish merchants.

Britain began ending the slave trade in the early 1800s. This evolved into a long and bitter conflict with the Ashanti. Britain defeated them in 1874. The coastal region became the British colony of the Gold Coast. After another conflict with the Ashanti erupted in 1896, their northern kingdom was absorbed into the Gold Coast in 1901.

The independence movement in Ghana gained huge momentum following World War II. The United Gold Coast Convention was formed by moderates in 1947. The breakaway Convention People's Party (CPP) was formed with Kwame Nkrumah as its leader. The CPP won internal self-government throughout the 1950s.

Ghana

Britain granted independence to the Gold Coast as the nation of Ghana on March 6, 1957. The name was derived from a kingdom that had once ruled in the north. Nkrumah was the first prime minister. He was elected president of the Republic of Ghana in 1960.

Four years later Nkrumah converted Ghana to a socialist, one-party state. He made himself president for life. The economy deteriorated rapidly. The president was overthrown in a military coup in 1966.

Kofi Busia was elected president of a new civilian government in 1969. Busia encountered the same increasing inflation and labor unrest which has plagued his predecessor. The army acted again in 1972, installing Lt. Col. Ignatius Acheampong as president. The new National Redemption Council had some success at stabilizing the economy.

Acheampong was deposed in 1978. He was replaced by Gen. Frederick Akuffo, who was later overthrown by Flight-Lieutenant Jerry Rawlings in January of 1979. Rawlings was determined to end the corruption. He had both of his predecessors executed. Rawlings stepped down in favor of Hilla Linman, an elected civilian president, in 1979.

The economy deteriorated further and unrest worsened. Rawlings became president again in 1981. The World Bank and International Monetary Fund provided aid which helped the economy improve throughout the 1990s.

A new constitution was adopted in 1992. Rawlings was twice elected president but had to step down in 2000, as required by the constitution. Opposition Leader John Agyekum Kufuor became president. It was the first peaceful transition from one president to another in Ghana's history.

Fort Metal Cross rises over the harbor at Dixcove in western Ghana.

LONELY PLANET IMAGES – ARIADNE VAN ZANDBERGEN

Greece

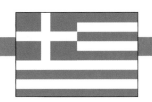

HELLENIC REPUBLIC

GOVERNMENT
Website
www.government.gr/english.html
Capital Athens
Type of government Republic
Independence from Ottoman Empire March 25, 1821
Voting
Universal adult suffrage, compulsory
Head of state President
Head of government Prime Minister
Constitution 1975 (revised 2001)
Legislature
Unicameral Parliament (Vouli ton Ellinon)
Judiciary Supreme Judicial Court
Member of
CE, EU, IMF, NATO, OECD, UN, UNESCO, UNHCR, WHO, WTO

LAND AND PEOPLE
Land area 50,949 sq mi (131,957 sq km)
Highest point Mount Olympus 9,570 ft (2, 917 m)
Coastline 8,498 ft (13,675 km)
Population 10,975,000
Major cities and populations
Athens 3,200,000
Thessalonika 745,000
Piraeus 202,000
Patras 175,000
Ethnic groups
Greek 95%, others 5%
Religions Christianity 95%
Languages Greek (official)

ECONOMIC
Currency Euro
Industry
tourism, food processing, textiles, chemicals, metal products, mining, petroleum refining
Agriculture
tobacco, wheat, corn, barley, beet sugar, olives, tomatoes, wine, potatoes; beef, dairy
Natural resources
bauxite, lignite, magnesite, petroleum, marble

Located in southeastern Europe, Greece occupies the southernmost part of the Balkan Peninsula. It is bordered on the north by Albania, Macedonia, Bulgaria and Turkey. Its coastline faces the Aegean Sea on the east, the Mediterranean Sea on the south and the Ionion Sea on the west. Greece has 1600 islands, including Crete. These islands make up about one-fifth of the country's total land mass. The Pindus Mountains run north to south, creating a rugged landscape in which few people live. Lower-lying regions are mainly found in the northeast, stretching from the Aegean to Macedonia. Only about thirty percent of the land is suitable for farming. Summers are dry and hot. Winters are cool to warm, except in the mountains where they can be very cold.

Ethnic Greeks make up more than ninety-five percent of the population. The balance is made up of immigrants from neighboring countries. Ninety-five percent of the people are Christians, primarily Greek Orthodox. Greek is the official language. Most people use the modern Demotike vernacular version of the language. Greece is the center of one of the world's oldest civilizations.

The Greek economy is based on agriculture, tourism, services and manufacturing. Primary crops include tobacco, wheat, tomatoes, citrus fruits, grapes, olives, wheat, barley, corn, potatoes, beet sugar and cotton.

The country has worked to build stronger industries since World War II. Manufacturing has matched agriculture in its importance to the economy since the 1970s. Leading fabricated items include metal products, processed foods, textiles, chemicals and clothing.

Tourism is a vital part of the country's economy. Greece's historical landscape, Mediterranean climate and its beautiful islands draw millions of tourists from around the world each year.

The current constitution came into effect in 1975. Greece's unicameral parliament has between 200 and 300 members. All are elected by proportional representation for four-year terms. The president, elected for a five-year term by members of the parliament, is head of state and commander of the armed forces. The president selects a prime minister who, in turn, selects cabinet members. The Council of the Republic, made up of present and former officials, advises the president.

Greek civilization can be traced back to about 4000 B.C. The Minoans, Europe's first truly advanced civilization, arose on the island of Crete in

Greece

The Parthenon in Athens typifies the grandeur of ancient Greece.

2300 B.C. It later spread to Mycenae on the mainland. The civilization was centered on Mycenae after 1500 B.C.

Various tribes invaded from Asia Minor, settling in different regions. The many small settlements developed systems of government. Some grew into powerful city-states, the largest of which were Athens and Sparta. Greek mariners established colonies on the shores of Africa, in Spain, France and Italy between the eighth and sixth centuries B.C.

Persia made major efforts to conquer Greece begining in the sixth century B.C. They were successful at capturing certain areas, including many of the islands in the Aegean Sea. The Athenians finally defeated the invaders with aid from the Spartans.

Athens emerged from the Persian wars as the most influential state in Greece. This marked the beginning of the golden age of Greek civilization, which has left an invaluable heritage of written history and language. Pericles, who became head of state in 460 B.C., supervised construction of many grand buildings including the Parthenon. He wanted Athens to be the most beautiful city in the world.

Sparta resented the influence and prosperity of Athens. A fierce struggle ensued. The Peloponnesian Wars began in 431 B.C. Sparta was victorious by 404 B.C. Athenians rebelled against the brutal Spartan control in a series of battles that continued well into the fourth century B.C.

Macedonian King Philip II had many victories over the city-states by 338 B.C. He laid the groundwork for his son Alexander the Great's era of conquests. Alexander took Greek civilization east to India, west into Europe and south to Egypt. Following his death, Alexander's generals battled for control of the empire between 322 B.C. and 275 B.C.

All of this fighting finally took its toll. As Greece declined, the Roman Empire began its spectacular rise. The Greek peninsula fell under Roman rule after the Fourth Macedonian War in 146 B.C. Although the various regions retained some independence, much of their culture merged with that of Rome.

The declining Roman Empire was divided into eastern and western regions in 395 A.D. The east, of which Greece was a part, became the Byzantine Empire. Centuries of invasions followed, starting with the Visigoths in 378 A.D. Between then and the ninth century, Greece was overrun by Huns, Avars, Bulgars and Slavs.

Franks leading the Fourth Crusade captured Constantinople in 1204 and changed the Byzantine Empire into the

The spectacular position and unique architecture of Santorini.

Latin Empire of the East. They divided Greece into small areas called 'fiefs.' The Latin Empire fell in 1261. Italian, French and Spanish rulers controlled Athens for the next two centuries.

Greece came under the control of the Ottoman Turks by 1460. Greek nationalism grew steadily under the Turks. Greek nationalists had an enthusiastic supporter in Tsar Alexander I of Russia. Financial backing came from various others European countries.

When the Greeks declared themselves independent on March 25, 1821, war broke out immediately with Turkey. Britain, France and Russia demanded an armistice in 1827. Turkey's refusal led to its defeat by a combined naval fleet. The European powers recognized Greek independence in 1832.

Prince Otto of Bavaria became the new King of Greece. His authoritarian rule proved unpopular, leading to his overthrow in 1862. Replacing him was another member of a European royal house, Prince William George of Denmark.

Greek territory expanded through the late nineteenth and early twentieth centuries. Macedonia, Crete, Epirus and the Ionian Islands were acquired after the Balkan Wars of 1912-13.

Greece

**Buying oranges at a
market stall in Athens.**

King George was assassinated at Salonika in 1913. His successor, King Constantine I, clashed with the government over neutrality in World War I. Prime Minister Eleutherios Venizelos, who backed the Allies, was dismissed by the king who favored neutrality. Venizelos then organized a rival government based at Thessalonika. International pressure forced Constantine to abdicate in favor of his son, Alexander in 1917.

Alexander died in 1920, to be replaced by his father, Constantine II. He was succeeded by King George II in 1922. George stepped down the following year when Greece was declared a republic by parliament. This began a period of numerous coups d'état as various political groups tried to gain control. The communists held the balance of power in parliament by 1935. Prime Minister Joannis Metaxis established a fascist dictatorship, in an attempt to prevent a communist takeover.

Despite claiming neutrality in World War II, Greece was invaded by Italy in October of 1940. The assault was repelled, but a vastly superior German army had gathered on the Greek border. In April of 1941 a force of British troops arrived to aid Greece. They were soundly defeated by the Germans.

The Greek government fled to Crete and later to Cairo with the evacuating troops. It established a government-in-exile in London. Resistance continued through the bleak years of German occupation. It was led by the communist National Liberation Front (EAM) and the monarchist Free Democratic Greek Party (EDES).

When the Germans were driven out in October of 1944 by British troops, the EAM and the EDES launched a civil war for control of the nation. The EAM clashed with British forces when it failed to disarm. A truce was arranged in February of 1945. The people voted in 1946 to reinstate George II as monarch.

Civil war continued. The communists received aid from the Soviet Union. By 1947 the United States was pouring military and economic aid into Greece to help defeat the communists. The royalists gained control in 1949. The civil war created long-lasting divisions in Greek society.

Conservative political parties held power through the 1950s. In 1964 George Papandreou led his centrist Union Party to power with a huge majority. He resigned the following year over claims that left-wing military officers were planning a coup d'état. A period of great instability followed.

On April 21, 1967, before new elections could be held, a group of right-wing military officers staged a coup. They claimed it was to prevent a communist takeover. Led by Lt.-Col. Georgios Papadopoulos, the new regime launched a brutal crackdown on leftist groups. Parliament was suspended. Violations of human rights were widespread.

King Constantine attempted a counter-coup in December. He went into exile in Rome after this attempt failed. His continued plotting for a return to the previous system prompted the military to declare a republic in 1973 with Papadopoulos as president.

A student uprising in November 1973 led to another military coup d'état. General Demitrios Ioannides deposed Papadopoulos to become president. The regime was eventually brought down by its attempts to interfere in the government of Cyprus, which had suffered an invasion by Turkey.

A civilian government was restored in 1974. It was led by Constantine Karamanlis. The 1951 constitution was reinstated, though the Greek people voted against restoration of the monarchy.

Greece joined the European Union in 1981. The economy remained weak through the 1980s due to the inefficiency of state-run businesses. Large-scale privatization began after Constantine Mitsotakis became prime minister in 1990.

Kostis Stephanopolous was elected president in 1995 and again in 2000. Greece continues to work on improving relations with Turkey and Macedonia.

The ruins of the Temple of Zeus in Athens.

Grenada

STATE OF GRENADA

Grenada is located in the southeastern Caribbean Sea. It is the southern-most of the Windward Islands. It includes the main island plus the Southern Grenadines to the northwest. On the main island a volcanic mountain ridge runs from north to south. Beautiful fertile valleys are crossed by streams of spring waters. The southern coast is a string of sandy beaches. Grenada's climate is subtropical. The wet season lasts from June to December.

Most of the population is of African origin. There are a small number of mixed race people and a tiny minority of Europeans. The islands are pre-dominantly Christian. English is the official language.

Agriculture, in the form of small farms, is most important to Grenada's economy. Crops include fruits, cacao, coconut, bananas, cotton, and spices. Tourism is becoming increas-ingly essential to the country's livelihood.

Grenada was populated by Carib indigenous peoples when Christopher Columbus arrived in 1498. They fiercely resisted all attempts at colonization by Europeans. Eventually, they were exterminated by French settlers in the 1650s.

French possession of the island was disputed by Britain. British colonialists finally secured control in 1762 and this annexation was confirmed in 1783. British settlers moved in to establish sugar cane plan-tations. Large numbers of Africans were brought in to work as forced laborers.

Britain gave the island full internal self-government in 1967. Independence was granted on February 7, 1974, with Eric Gairy as the first prime minister. The British monarch remained head of state. Gairy was deposed in a 1979 coup d'état headed by Maurice Bishop, a supporter of Cuban president Fidel Castro. They established the People's Revolutionary Government with Maurice Bishop as prime minis-ter.

Bishop and others were mur-dered by hard-line radicals in a coup in 1983. The governor-gen-eral called for outside interven-tion. The United States, aided by a contingent from the Organi-zatin of East Caribbean States, invaded the island. They secured control of Grenada in a relatively short time, but secu-rity advisors remained.

Herbert Blaize was elected prime minister in 1984. There has been no reoccurrence of the earlier radical movements. Multi-party elections continue. In subsequent decades Grenada's recent involvement in international banking has brought it into public scrunity for possible participation in ille-gal activities.

GOVERNMENT
Capital St. George's
Type of government
Parliamentary democracy
Independence from Britain
February 7, 1974
Voting Universal adult suffrage
Head of state
British Crown,
represented by Governor-General
Head of government Prime Minister
Constitution 1973
Legislature
Bicameral Parliament
House of Representatives (lower house), Senate (upper house)
Judiciary West Indies Associate States Supreme Court
Member of Caricom, CN, IMF, OAS, UN, UNESCO, WHO, WTO

LAND AND PEOPLE
Land area 121 sq mi (311 sq km)
Highest point
Mount Saint Catherine
2,275 ft (840 m)
Coastline 75 mi (121 km)
Population 89,227
Major cities and populations
St George's 35,472
Ethnic groups African 84%,
Mulatto 12%, indigenous 3%,
European 1%
Religions Christianity
Languages
English (official), French-African patois

ECONOMIC
Currency East Caribbean dollar
Industry
food, beverages, textiles,
light assembly, tourism
Agriculture
bananas, cocoa, nutmeg, mace,
citrus, avocados, root crops, sugar cane, corn, vegetables
Natural resources
timber, tropical fruit

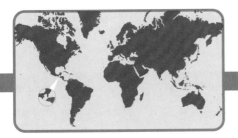

Guatemala

REPUBLIC OF GUATEMALA

GOVERNMENT
Website www.guatemala.gob.gt
Capital Guatemala City
Type of government Republic
Independence from Spain
September 15, 1821
Voting Universal adult suffrage
Head of state President
Head of government President
Constitution 1985
Legislature
Unicameral Congress of the
Republic
Judiciary Supreme Court of
Justice
Member of
IMF, OAS, UN, UNESCO, WHO,
WTO

LAND AND PEOPLE
Land area
42,042 sq mi (108,889 sq km)
Highest point
Volcan Tajumulco 13,815 ft (4211 m)
Coastline 250 mi (402 km)
Population 13,314,079
Major cities and populations
Guatemala City 1,200,000
Mixco 450,000
Villa Nueva 172,000
Ethnic groups
Mestizos 60%, Maya 39%
Religions
Christianity 98%, Mayan faiths 2%
Languages
Spanish (official), indigenous
languages

ECONOMIC
Currency Quetzal
Industry
sugar refining, textiles, clothing,
furniture, chemicals, petroleum,
mining, rubber, tourism
Agriculture
sugar cane, corn, bananas, coffee,
beans, cardamom, cattle, sheep,
pigs, poultry
Natural resources
petroleum, nickel, timber, seafood

Guatemala is located in Central America. Its southwest coastline fronts the Pacific Ocean, with a low-lying and very fertile plain. It has a narrower coastline in the northeast on the Caribbean Sea. The Petén Tableland lies in the north. Mountain runs from the northwest to the southeast through the center, with two main volcanic ranges. Guatemala is tropical with little variation in temperatures throughout the year. A rainy season occurs between May and October.

Over half of Guatemala's people are mestizos, with combined Spanish and Mayan backgrounds. Most of the others are indigenous Maya, with tiny European and African minorities. Some indigenous people follow Mayan religious practices. The rest of the population is Christian. While Spanish is the official language, there are twenty indigenous dialects.

The Mayan people had a rich and vibrant civilization in what is now Guatemala. It began before 1500 B.C. and thrived until about A.D. 900, when it went into decline.

The remaining Maya put up a spirited fight against the Spanish invaders led by Pedro de Alvarado in 1523. The intruders prevailed and the land became Spanish territory. Disappointed to find no gold, the Spanish began cultivating indigo and cocoa. Indigenous people were recruited as forced laborers.

Guatemala declared its independence from Spain in 1821. It was briefly part of the Mexican Empire. It then joined the ill-fated Central American Federation. Rafael Carrera, a Guatemalan, began a peasants' revolt in 1838. This led to the federation's demise.

Carrera became the first Guatemalan president in 1840. He remained in the post for twenty-seven years. Under Carrera and his successors, Guatemala was notorious for interfering in the affairs of

Colourful craft works on sale at a market in Castillo San Felipe.

BRAND X PICTURES

Guatemala

neighboring countries. Guatemalan governments were dictatorships until 1920.

A new government elected in 1920 was overthrown in a coup d'état the following year. Two succeeding governments also ended abruptly.

Jorge Ubico came to power, supported by the coffee and banana planters, in 1931. He outlawed trade unions and left-wing political parties. The economy thrived under Ubico. He was overthrown in 1944, due to his harsh exercise of power.

His successor, Juan José Arevalo Bermejo, reinstated trade unions and began a program of social and economic reform. Guatemala came into dispute over control of British Honduras during this time.

Col. Jacobo Arbenz Guzman became president in 1951. Under his reform policies, large tracts of land were confiscated from powerful companies such as the American-owned United

A Mayan structure at Tikal

Fruit. International concern grew as Arbenz appeared determined to set up a communist government. The United States supported the military coup which overthrew him.

Colonel Castillo Armas, reversed most of Arbenz's reforms before he was assassinated in 1957. Left-wing military officers and politicians formed guerrilla groups to challenge the military leaderships that followed. Many of these people were killed during a 1968 anti-guerrilla campaign.

Gen. Carlos Arana Osorio, a hard-line conservative, became president in 1970. He applied even harsher measures against anyone who opposed the government. His successor, Gen. Kjell Eugenio Luagerud Garcia, continued these practices.

Guerrilla action gathered momentum in the 1980s under the banner of the Guatemalan

National Revolutionary Unity. Various military coups were attempted in the late 1980s but all failed. From the early 1960s to the mid-1990s, 100,000 people were killed in civil wars, while 40,000 others simply disappeared.

Changes finally came in 1996 when civilian Álvaro Arzú Irigoyen was elected president. He purged the higher ranks of the military and signed a United Nations peace accord with the guerillas. Power switched back to the conservatives in 1999, when Alfonso Potrillo Cabrera became president and the Guatemalan Republican Front took control of the legislature.

The idyllic Guatemalan coastline at Honduras Bay.

Guinea

REPUBLIC OF GUINEA

GOVERNMENT
Website www.guinee.gov.gn
Capital Conakry
Type of government Republic
Independence from France
October 2, 1958
Voting Universal adult suffrage
Head of state President
Head of government Prime
Minister
Constitution 1990
Legislature
Unicameral People's National
Assembly
Judiciary Court of Appeal
Member of IMF, OAU, UN,
UNESCO, WHO, WTO

LAND AND PEOPLE
Land area 94,926 sq mi
(245,857 sq km)
Highest point Mont Nimba
6,070 ft (1,850 m)
Coastline 199 mi (320 km)
Population 7,775,065
Major cities and populations
Conakry 1,824,000
Kankan 85,000
Ethnic groups
Fulani 40%, Malinké 26%, Susu
10%, Kissi 6%, Kpelle 5%, others
13%
Religions Islam 85%, traditional
animism 10%, Christianity 5%
Languages
French (official), indigenous
languages

ECONOMIC
Currency Guinean franc
Industry
mining, alumina refining; light
manufacturing, agricultural
processing
Agriculture
rice, coffee, pineapples, palm
kernels, tapioca, bananas, sweet
potatoes, cattle, sheep, goats, timber
Natural resources
bauxite, iron ore, diamonds, gold,
uranium, seafood

Located in western Africa, Guinea has a wide coastal plain that extends from the Atlantic Ocean. Inland, the landscape rises to the Futa Jallon highlands. The interior is predominantly grassland, while the extreme southeast is heavily forested. The tropical climate brings high temperatures and humidity year round.

Forty percent of Guinea's population are the Fulani. Other large groups include the Malinké and the Susu. Islam is the dominant religion. While French is the official language, at least eight regional indigenous languages are also spoken. Most people in Guinea live as farmers. Guinea remains a very poor country. Ample mineral deposits have yet to be mined.

In the ninth century A.D., Susu tribes arrived from northern deserts, driving the indigenous Baga people to the coastal areas. Fulani conquered the Futa Jallon region in the sixteenth century. In 1725 they began aggressively converting the region to Islam.

France and Portugal began seizing people from Guinea who were sold into slavery during the 1600s. Palm oil and peanuts became important commodities of trade with the Europeans. France declared the Boké region a protectorate in 1849 when French traders rebelled against levies charged by local tribes.

Using conquest and negotiation, France came to dominate all of Guinea. It was made a French colony. Opposition to French rule continued into the twentieth century. Guinea became part of the French West African Federation in 1906.

Unlike other French colonies, Guinea opted for total independence on October 2, 1958. The first president was Ahmed Sékou Touré. France withdrew all aid, forcing Guinea to approach the Soviet Union for help.

Touré banned all opposition political parties. He engineered a largely symbolic union with Ghana and Mali. Relations with most other countries were severed. This ultimately brought economic hardship to Guinea. Touré tried to reestablish international ties and to liberalize his government.

Touré died in March 1984 and Col. Lansana Conté became president. His Military Committee of National Recovery adopted a new constitution in 1990. Conté freed political prisoners, improved foreign relations and began dismantling the socialist system.

Conté was elected in 1993 and again in 1998. Half a million refugees fled into Guinea to escape wars in Sierra Leone and Liberia in the late 1990s. This has added to its problems.

Guinea-Bissau

REPUBLIC OF GUINEA-BISSAU

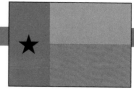

Fronting the Atlantic Ocean, Guinea-Bissau is located in western Africa. Most of the country is low-lying swampy coastal plain. The land rises in the northeast to a grassland plateau. High humidity and high temperatures prevail throughout the year.

Only twenty percent of the people live in urban areas. Most people live and work on farms. The larger ethnic groups are the Balante, Fulani, Mandyako, Malinke and Pepel. More than half of the people practice traditional animist religions. Thirty percent are Muslims. The official language is Portugese.

Most of Guinea-Bissau's natural resources remain untapped. Tropical hardwoods and minerals such as bauxite, phosphate, zinc and copper, as well as offshore petroleum, could be exploited. According to a United Nations data, Guinea-Bissau is the poorest country in the world.

The Balante and Pepel had established civilizations in Guinea-Bissau as early as the twelfth century A.D. The Portuguese arrived in 1446. They began trading in slaves for their plantations in Brazil. The British and French also traded in slaves during the seventeenth and eighteenth centuries.

The region became the colony of Portuguese Guinea in 1879. Various border disputes with France occurred before clear control was emerged in 1915. It was named an overseas province in 1952.

The indigenous peoples continued to resist Portuguese occupation until the 1930s. The African Party for the Indepence of Guinea-Bissau and Cape Verde Islands (PAIGC) launched an armed campaign in 1962.

With three-quarters of the colony under its control, PAIGC declared independence in 1973. Luiz Cabral was named as president. Portugal formally granted independence in 1974.

Under the PAIGC, Guinea-Bissau was a one-party state. Cabral established a trade monopoly. He nationalized all landholdings. He was deposed in a coup in 1980 by João Bernardo Viera. Although just as repressive as the old, the new regime introduced a number of social changes. When the one-party state was revoked in 1994, Viera became president in Guinea-Bissau's first free elections.

An army mutiny in June 1998 evolved into full-scale civil war. Senegal and Guinea intervened to assist the president. The next year a military coup installed Malam Bacai Sanhá as president. In the January 2000 elections, Kuma Yalá was elected president. The army again rebelled but was quickly suppressed later in the year.

GOVERNMENT
Capital Bissau
Type of government Republic
Independence from Portugal
September 24, 1973
Voting Universal adult suffrage
Head of state President
Head of government Prime Minister
Constitution 1984
Legislature
Unicameral National People's Assembly
Judiciary Supreme Court
Member of IMF, OAU, UN, UNESCO, WHO, WTO

LAND AND PEOPLE
Land area 13,948 sq mi (36,125 sq km)
Highest point 948 ft (300 m)
Coastline 217 mi (350 km)
Population 1,345,479
Major cities and populations
Bissau 200,000
Bolama 27,000
Ethnic groups
Balante 30%, Fulani 20%, Mandyako 14%, Malinke 13%, Pepel 7%, others 16%
Religions Traditional animism 54%, Islam 38%, Christianity 8%
Languages
Portuguese (official), Portugese Creole

ECONOMIC
Currency CFA franc
Industry
agricultural processing, beverages
Agriculture
rice, corn, beans, tapioca, nuts, palm kernels, cotton, timber; seafood
Natural resources
seafood, timber, phosphates, bauxite, petroleum

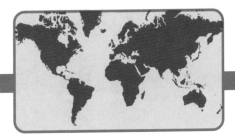

Guyana

COOPERATIVE REPUBLIC OF GUYANA

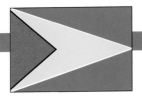

GOVERNMENT
Capital Georgetown
Type of government Republic
Independence from Britain
May 26, 1966
Voting Universal adult suffrage
Head of state President
Head of government Prime
Minister
Constitution 1980
Legislature
Unicameral National Assembly
Judiciary Supreme Court of
Judicature
Member of Caricom, CN, IMF,
OAS, UN, UNESCO, WHO, WTO

LAND AND PEOPLE
Land area 83,000 sq mi
(214,969 sq km)
Highest point Mount Roraima
9,301 ft (2,835 m)
Coastline 285 mi (459 km)
Population 698,209
Major cities and populations
Georgetown 260,000
Linden 35,000
Ethnic groups Indian 51%,
African-Indian 40%, indigenous 9%
Religions
Christianity 60%, Hinduism 30%,
Islam 10%
Languages
English (official), Hindi, Urdu

ECONOMIC
Currency Guyana dollar
Industry
mining, sugar refining, rice milling,
timber, textiles
Agriculture
sugar, rice, wheat, vegetable oils,
beef, pork, poultry, dairy, seafood
Natural resources
bauxite, gold, diamonds, hardwood
timber, seafood

Guyana is on the northeastern coast of South America. Its fertile coastal plain is heavily cultivated. Thick forests dominate three-fourths of the country. Guyana has numerous rivers which feature some of the most dramatic waterfalls on earth. High temperatures and humidity prevail throughout the year.

About half of Guyana's people are descended from Indian immigrants. Forty percent have African or mixed African-indigenous heritage. Christianity and Hinduism are the dominant religions. English is the official language, but Urdu, Hindi and other dialects are also spoken.

The region now known as Guyana was inhabited for centuries by Caribs, Warrau, Arawaks and Akawaios. Dutch explorers and settlers prevailed over the Spanish and British. Their plantations produced sugar, cotton and coffee using African slave labor.

British claims on the region failed when the 1667 Treaty of Breda awarded it to the Netherlands. The British gained formal possession in the early 1800s, but the Dutch remained until the British colony was named British Guiana in 1831.

The population of indigenous people continued to decline under British rule. Large numbers of people came from Africa and East India.

Britain granted Guiana internal self-government in 1961. The People's Progressive Party, under Cheddi Jagan, gained a legislative majority. Jagan began a program of economic reform, which resulted in violent riots. British troops were called in to quell the riots. Much of the strife was caused by disagreements between Africans and Indian supporters of Jagan.

On May 26, 1966, the colony, renamed Guyana, became independent. Forbes Burnham was elected prime minister. It was declared a socialist republic four years later. Guyana established relations with China and other Communist nations.

The People's Temple religious cult, led by Jim Jones, was established in the Guyana jungle in the 1970s. At Jones's instruction, 900 members committed suicide in 1978, creating an international sensation.

Burnham was elected president in 1980. He restricted press freedom and crushed any opposition. After Burnham's death in 1985, President Desmond Hoyte reversed previous socialist policies to encourage foreign investors.

Former Finance Minister Bharrat Jagdeo was elected president in 2001. Guyana has recovered from its socialist experiment. Its economic growth continues.

Haiti

REPUBLIC OF HAITI

Haiti shares the Caribbean island of Hispaniola with the Dominican Republic, occupying the western third. It consists of two peninsulas, each of which has a mountain range and many small valleys. The coastlines have numerous beautiful harbors. Many short, swift rivers run from the mountains. The climate is tropical, with high humidity and high temperatures in the lowlands. Mountain areas are cooler.

Haiti is Latin America's poorest country. Over ninety percent of the people are of African descent. The rest have African–French mulatto heritage. Most people are Christian. Traditional African religions have merged with Christian rites to create Voodoo for which Haiti is famous. French is the official language, but a French-Haitian Creole is most commonly spoken.

Arawaks were Haiti's indigenous people when Columbus arrived in 1492, naming the island Hispaniola. The Spanish colonized the east but left the west to French and British pirates in the seventeenth century. French settlers established sugar plantations using African slave labor.

The Treaty of Ryswick ceded the western third of Hispaniola to France in 1697. Named Saint-Domingue, it quickly prospered, producing coffee and sugar. A rebellion erupted when planters attempted to prevent people of mixed race from having representation in France's National Assembly.

England captured Haiti in 1793, during the Napoleonic Wars. Spain ceded its part of Hispaniola to France in 1795. Local guerrilla forces led by Toussaint L'Ouverture captured the former Spanish territory. He proclaimed himself governor-general of the island.

A huge French force recaptured some territory in 1802. Toussaint died in prison after being tricked into surrendering. The rebels were eventually successful, with United States help. A yellow fever epidemic that raged through the French forces also aided the rebels.

Haiti became the world's only independent black republic in 1804. French and Creole settlers were expelled. Jean-Jacques Dessalines, a former slave, declared himself

Pakistani peacekeeping troops patrol the streets of Port-au-Prince.

emperor. Haiti was split into northern and southern kingdoms after his 1806 assassination. It was reunified in 1822.

Nicolas Fabre Geffrard restored Haiti to republican government in 1859. The military and politicians vied for power and racial friction continued.

The United States intervened in 1915 to restore order. Philippe Sudre Dartiguenave became president. The United States provided a treaty assuring ten years of economic and political aid to help the government. A revolt against U. S. authority was put down in 1920. The treaty was extended for another ten years, but hostility against the U. S. continued. The U. S. military was withdrawn in 1934.

Under President Elie Lescot, Haiti participated in World War II on behalf of the Allies. A joint program between the United States and Haiti helped generate new crops for the impoverished country during the war. Haiti was a founding member of the United Nations in 1945.

Francois Duvalier was elected president in 1957. He organized the Tonton Macoute, an army which brutally eliminated opposition to his government. He declared himself president for life in 1964. The United States ended economic aid to Haiti in 1961 in response to Duvalier's methods. Duvalier's son, Jean-Claude succeeded him. Cor-

ruption and brutal repression continued. Jean-Claude was forced to flee the country in 1986.

The following years brought failed governments, military coups and contested elections. Jean-Bertrand Aristide was elected president in 1990, but he was deposed by the military in 1991.

The U. S. and the Organization of American States imposed trade sanctions on Haiti. The United Nations organized an oil embargo. The United Nations authorized outside military force when a 1993 agreement permitting Aristide's return was broken by the military.

Thousands of U. S. troops landed and established order on September 19, 1994. The mission was successful, largely because of diplomatic initiatives by former US President Jimmy Carter. Aristide returned to Haiti in October.

United Nations peacekeepers arrived in March of the following year. René Préval was elected president in December of 1995. Préval dismissed the legislature in 1999 and ruled by decree. The U. S. suspended its aid program.

In June 2000 Aristide's party gained control of the legislature. He was again elected president in November of the same year. That election had been boycotted by opposition parties.

GOVERNMENT
Website www.haiti.org
Capital Port-au-Prince
Type of government Republic
Independence from France
January 1, 1804
Voting Universal adult suffrage
Head of state President
Head of government Prime Minister
Constitution 1987
Legislature
Bicameral National Assembly
Chamber of Deputies (lower house), Senate (upper house)
Judiciary Supreme Court
Member of Caricom, IMF, OAS, UN, UNESCO, WHO, WTO

LAND AND PEOPLE
Land area 10,714 sq mi (27,750 sq km)
Highest point Chaine de la Selle 8,793 ft (2,680 m)
Coastline 1,100 mi (1,771 km)
Population 6,808,205
Major cities and populations
Port-au-Prince 1,500,000
Carrefour 280,000
Delmas 240,000
Ethnic groups African 95%, Mulatto 4%, European 1%
Religions Christianity, Voodoo
Languages
French (official), French-Haitian Creole

ECONOMIC
Currency Gourde
Industry
sugar refining, flour milling, textiles, cement, light assembly
Agriculture
coffee, mangoes, sugar cane, rice, corn, sorghum, timber
Natural resources
bauxite, copper, calcium carbonate, gold, marble

Honduras

REPUBLIC OF HONDURAS

Located in Central America, Honduras has two coastlines. It is bounded on the northeast by the Caribbean Sea, and on the southwest by the Pacific Ocean. Much of its landscape is a broad fertile plateau, crossed by mountain ranges in the west. The climate is tropical with regular, substantial rainfall on the Caribbean coast.

The population consists mainly of mestizos, people of mixed indigenous and European background. The other ten percent are Caribs, Africans and a small number of Europeans. The population is overwhelmingly Christian. The official language is Spanish.

Indigenous Hondurans can trace their roots back to 1700 B.C. The Mayan civilization flourished through the tenth century.

Christopher Columbus sighted the coastline in 1502. Spain began establishing mining centers in 1524. They crushed resistance by indigenous peoples, only to find very little gold in Honduras. Most people lived as farmers or ranchers in following years.

When independence came in 1821, Honduras was briefly part of the Mexican Empire. It joined the Central American Federation in 1825. Honduras was complelely independent by 1840. The rest of the century was marked by weak govern-

ments, both conservative and liberal.

The United Fruit Company and others established vast banana plantations in the 1800s. These organizations grew to have huge power. They built great ports and transportation routes, but they did little to aid the country's poor.

The first half of the twentieth century brought consistent political upheaval. Liberal President Ramón Villeda Morales, elected in 1957, initiated agricultural and educational reforms. He was ousted in a 1963 coup d'état.

Honduras declared war on El Salvador in 1969, in response to heavy immigration from that nation. The war lasted just two weeks, but it further harmed Honduras' fragile economy.

Under pressure from the United States, free elections were held in 1982. Robert Suaza Córdova became president, but the military retained much influence. Honduras became a base for thousands of guerrilas trying to overthrow Nicaragua's leftist government.

United States aid continued through the 1990s. A severe hurricane killed 5,600 people, destroyed homes, bridges, and caused nearly a billion dollars damage to farms in October of 1998. President Ricardo Maduro was elected in 2001. He has pledged to fight poverty and crime.

GOVERNMENT
Capital Tegucigalpa
Type of government Republic
Independence from Spain
September 15, 1821
Voting
Universal adult suffrage, compulsory
Head of state President
Head of government President
Constitution 1982
Legislature
Unicameral National Congress
Judiciary Supreme Court of Justice
Member of
IMF, OAS, UN, UNESCO, WHO, WTO

LAND AND PEOPLE
Land area 43,277 sq mi (112,088 sq km)
Highest point Cerro Las Minas 9,416 ft (2,870 m)
Coastline 1,130 mi (1,820 km)
Population 6,560,608
Major cities and populations
Tegucigalpa 850,000
San Pedro Sula 390,000
La Ceiba 95,000
Ethnic groups
Mestizos 90%, indigenous 7%, African 2%, European 1%
Religions Christianity
Languages
Spanish (official), indigenous languages

ECONOMIC
Currency Lempira
Industry
sugar refining, food processing, textiles, clothing, wood products
Agriculture
bananas, coffee, citrus, beef, timber, seafood
Natural resources
timber, gold, silver, copper, lead, zinc, iron ore, antimony, coal, seafood